THE HILLS

Lessons in Love

LILA STEWART

POCKET BOOKS / MTV BOOKS

NEW YORK   LONDON   TORONTO   SYDNEY

Pocket Books
A Division of Simon & Schuster, Inc.
1230 Avenue of the Americas
New York, NY 10020

Press photographs by Jeff Lipsky

First MTV Books/Pocket Books trade paperback edition
November 2008

For information about special discounts for bulk purchases,
please contact Simon & Schuster Special Sales at
1-800-456-6798 or business@simonandschuster.com

Designed by Mary Austin Speaker

Manufactured in the United States of America

10 9 8 7 6 5 4 3 2 1

Library of Congress Cataloging-in-Publication Data

Stewart, Lila.
    The Hills: lessons in love/Lila Stewart.
        p. cm.
    1. Hills (Television program)   2. Dating (Social customs)
I. Title.
    PN1992.77.H54S84 2008
    791.45'72—dc22   2008021784

ISBN-13: 978-1-4165-9370-6
ISBN-10:   1-4165-9370-5

THE HILLS

Lessons in Love

INTRODUCTION

Ever since the hit reality series *The Hills* debuted in the spring of 2006, Lauren, Whitney, Audrina, and Heidi have become like best friends to their fans. And just as with our best friends, we've also figured out their personalities. Lauren is hardworking, putting in long hours at fashion school and *Teen Vogue*. Fun-loving Heidi dropped out of school after only one class and instead rocks the party circuit as a successful promoter. While elegant Whitney would look as natural in a couture gown as she does in a bathrobe, Audrina generally prefers leather and motorcycles. The girls are gorgeous, rich, and living the high life in the Hills, but like any of us, they know what they absolutely adore and what they can't stand—especially from guys.

Just as the girls have their unique styles with clothes, work, and friends, they also have their own distinct styles when it comes to romance. To help you figure out your own approach to dating, try thinking about which of the four girls is most like you. Are you a Lauren—turning down an amazing job in Paris to spend the summer with your boyfriend? Or maybe you're an Audrina—you just can't keep away from that irresistible bad boy who makes you want to jump all over him one day and fight with him the next.

Whichever girl you relate to most, there's a pretty good chance you could use some dating advice— couldn't we all? Luckily, Lauren, Audrina, Whitney, and Heidi have done the hard work already. They've scouted the best guy-spotting places, sat through the excruciating blind dates, and heard the worst—really the worst—pickup lines in the world. Now, they're going to offer the fruits of that wisdom, so we don't have to make the same mistakes they did. And they'll be the first to admit—there were plenty of mistakes.

The dating world can be rough sometimes, so just

like the girls of *The Hills*, you'll need a dating strategy—
and this book offers four of them. But before you
plunge in, the first thing to figure out is . . . are you a
Lauren, an Audrina, a Whitney, or a Heidi?

IDENTIFY
YOURSELF

Different Girls Date Differently

●　●

Now for the hard talk . . . if you're looking for that one, mysterious "secret" to dating—then you can just close this book right now and go look somewhere else. In case you haven't figured it out yet, dating is complicated, guys are complicated—girls are complicated—so why do we expect dating strategy to be simple?

That doesn't mean that figuring out what you want

and don't want from guys has to be some long, arduous process. This is dating, not trekking through Siberia! It's just that sometimes knowing what you want from guys means knowing yourself. That takes a little soul-searching. Lauren, Whitney, Audrina, and Heidi are our dating guides, but they're just girls too. In the end, you're going to have to figure out what you want. And you're the only one who can do that.

But first, let's take a deeper look at the four girls, so you can see whom you relate to best. Are you a Lauren, a Whitney, an Audrina, or a Heidi?

IF YOU'RE A LAUREN...

You're hard-working, responsible, and sponsible, and driven. You set clear, ambitious goals for yourself, and you don't give up until they become a reality.

If you had your choice, you'd rather go to dinner with a small group of your close friends than hang out at a party with a bunch of people you just met. Loyalty is huge with you. You love your close friends, and they know exactly how you feel about them. They can rely on you, and you expect the same from them.

You like to go out and have fun, but you don't let partying get in the way of doing well at work. When a big project is done, you have no problem going out with your friends to celebrate, but you wait until *after* meeting the big deadline, not before.

For a Lauren, the world of dating is both a challenge and a thrill. At times you find it fun and exciting, and at other times it's confusing and frustrating. You go out on your share of dates, but you tend to know right away when a guy isn't right for you. And you're not going to stick with a guy who doesn't interest you. Let's face it, you get bored easily. When a guy isn't right, you're the type to make a *polite* excuse and end the date early—you don't want to hurt his feelings, but you also don't want to waste your evening!

Your casual relationships don't tend to last long, but when you're in a serious relationship, you throw everything you have into it, and you never hold anything back. You're a firm believer in true love, and you give your whole heart without fear of the consequences. As a result, you've had your heart broken a few times, but you're just not the type to be guarded or reserved when it comes to romance.

IF YOU'RE A WHITNEY...

You know who you are and what you believe in. You know exactly how you want to be treated, and any guy who doesn't respect that won't last too long. In your opinion, being in a relation- ship doesn't mean chang- ing who you are as a person—if a guy doesn't like you as you are, he can go find another girl.

For a Whitney, love is serious business. You're not much interested in casual dating or hook- ing up, and bad boys who might be good for a fling just aren't your thing. You want to date guys who are inter- ested in a long-term girlfriend. You'd rather go for a long walk to get to know someone than try to shout over people in a noisy club. You're careful and cautious before diving into a new relationship. When you're first getting to know someone, you take things slowly.

When you finally decide to take the plunge with a new relationship, things tend to get serious quickly. You want what you have with your new guy to be

exclusive—that means you and only you—and you expect him to feel the same way. When you're in a relationship, you like to share your feelings—if your new
guy can't be honest, he better figure out how fast. You
have no patience for playing games.

You are a loving and committed girlfriend, and you
demand the same in return. While you are trusting and
laid-back, you don't give your boyfriends a lot of room
to screw around. You know that without trust, no relationship can survive. Secrets and lies have no place in
the relationship of a Whitney.

IF YOU'RE AN
AUDRINA...

You like what you like, you
know what you like, and
there's not a whole lot
anyone else can say about it.
What other people like isn't very interesting to you. What other people *think* you
should like isn't interesting at all.

You have a big group of friends in your life, and

that's the way you like it. You're definitely at home in the club scene and can't think of a better way to spend a night than rocking it out on the dance floor. You don't spend a lot of time judging yourself, and you're not much interested in judging your friends either. In your opinion, everyone should live her life the way she wants—you certainly do! You're really not into a whole lot of drama. When it comes to fights, you'd rather just let things slide instead of making a big deal out of them. One exception: your friends. They all know that when they're in trouble, an Audrina will have their back—no matter what!

Still, as much as you value your friends, you can't always please them. You're more than happy to listen to their advice, but in the end you like to do things your way—and sometimes that's not *their* way. If Lauren thinks a certain guy isn't good enough for you, you'll listen to her thoughts. But you might still go out with him—after all, *you* like him, and that's what matters.

You're a bit of an alternative girl and you like your guys to match. You usually go for the arty guys, even when your friends think they're too scruffy. To an Audrina, ordinary, preppy types are just boring. You've learned the hard way, though, how it feels to be abandoned—rebels aren't usually the most reliable boyfriends. But in the end, it doesn't matter. You're the type who would rather risk the deep lows of arguments and slammed doors if you can also have the highs of wild motorcycle rides and after-hours dips in the ocean. You're not going to choose a boring guy simply because he's a safe bet, and you're not going to pretend to love somebody just to please your friends.

IF YOU'RE A HEIDI...

You've never had trouble with guys—for you, scoring dates has always been as easy as scoring shoes. You're always ready to have fun, whether it's at a club, at a party, or just lounging at home, and guys love that about you. What's more, you've never had any trouble getting boys to do what you want—you can be very persuasive!

You've got the reputation as a party girl who can flirt with one guy at a club while getting another one to buy you a drink. But even though you might have looked and acted like a player, in your heart you're really just waiting for that one special someone to come along and sweep you off your feet.

When you do find your prince, a Heidi is in no hurry to wait. If the guy is right for you, you're ready to get serious: move in together, even get engaged! You've already figured out what you want, so why wait? When other girls are reaching for the brakes, you're just shifting into third gear.

Of course, not every guy can keep up with all your energy, so you don't waste your time with wimpy guys who stand in the corner waiting for something to happen. Your ideal type is a male version of you: ambitious, assertive, loud, funny. You won't settle until you meet your match.

A Heidi isn't one to hide her feelings: you always tell your boyfriend exactly how you feel. Whether it's poetry, love letters, or the last thing he hears before he goes to sleep, your emotions are never a secret. After all, you love the guy, so why not tell him?

Once you've scored an amazing guy, you're reluctant to let him go—in fact, you'd rather spend time with him than with anyone else. You *can* be possessive—even thinking of your guy with another girl makes you sick. When you're in a relationship, you don't have a lot of time for your old friends, but this is a price you're happy to pay.

THE WHILAURDRINEIDI QUIZ

Still haven't pegged yourself as a Lauren, Whitney, Audrina, or Heidi? Take this quiz.

Are you the type of girl who'd go out with a guy just for his smile or break up with a boy just for his bad breath? Was your first kiss an epic romantic moment, or a symphony of awkwardness? What do you lie to boys about?

Take this quiz, and choose the answers that best apply to you and your life. Then check your answers to see whom you most resemble.

1. What's your perfect date?
    (a) Takeout and a DVD—quiet and intimate
    (b) Going to a hockey game—nothing fancy
    (c) A guy cooking for you and sharing a bottle of wine—small and romantic
    (d) Getting dressed up and meeting a bunch of friends—big and festive
2. Who's your celebrity crush?
    (a) I don't like celebrities, I like real people
    (b) Mark Wahlberg
    (c) Ryan Gosling
    (d) Henry Cavill

3. What's your favorite romantic movie?

   (a) *The Notebook*

   (b) *Love Actually*

   (c) *Moulin Rouge!*

   (d) *Dirty Dancing*

4. What's the most romantic place in the world?

   (a) Cabo San Lucas

   (b) A night on the beach

   (c) Paris

   (d) A sunset on the beach

5. What's your idea of a perfect Valentine's Day gift?

   (a) Diamonds

   (b) A self-made valentine

   (c) A handwritten letter

   (d) His singing me a song he wrote himself

6. I love a guy who wears . . .

   (a) A little scruff

   (b) Vintage clothing

   (c) Jeans and a T-shirt

   (d) Good-smelling cologne

7. The most important quality in a boyfriend is . . .

   (a) Thoughtfulness

   (b) His support

   (c) Being a good listener

   (d) Respect

8. I once dated a guy just for his . . .

   (a) Smile

   (b) Car

   (c) I always look for the total package

   (d) Looks

9. I once broke up with a guy just for his . . .

   (a) Odor

   (b) Laugh—it was the most annoying thing I ever heard

   (c) Bad breath

   (d) Bad attitude. I hate cocky

10. Most guys don't know I actually . . .

    (a) Am very silly

    (b) Know when they're lying to me

    (c) Am a really picky person

    (d) Love to ride motorcycles and dirt bikes

11. The cheesiest thing I ever said to a guy was . . .

    (a) "I'm going to marry you" (the first night I met him!)

    (b) "I like you. Do you like me?"

    (c) I've never used a cheesy line on a guy

    (d) "Is there an airport near here, or is that just my heart taking off?"

12. The cheesiest thing a guy ever said to me was . . .

    (a) "Click your heels, Dorothy, and land yourself in my bed!"

(b) "You have the most beautiful eyes" (after the hundredth time he said it)

(c) Guys don't really try those kinds of lines on me

(d) "Can I be the gravy on your biscuit?" "If there were a kiss for every snowflake, I would send you a blizzard" (tie)

13. My first kiss was . . .

(a) Cold

(b) Awful—he stuck his tongue down my throat, then told the school I was a horrible kisser

(c) Pretty awkward—it was in a limo after a tenth-grade formal. People were cheering

(d) Fantastic

14. I only lie to boys when talking about . . .

(a) Spending habits

(b) Exes and other boys

(c) I try not to lie, but sometimes bend the truth when they want to make plans

(d) My beauty secrets

ANSWER KEY: *a = Heidi, b = Lauren, c = Whitney, d = Audrina*

LOOKING
FOR LOVE

It's Not Where You Are, It's Who You Are

You know those girls who spend all evening getting ready to go out—everything waxed and shaved, hair blown out, perfect makeup, perfect bag, perfect shoes? And then they go to the party or the club or the restaurant and never meet anyone. But there's always that one girl—everyone knows her. She throws on a pair of jeans and a tank top and puts her *hair up in a bun, and within five minutes of entering the club, three guys are trying to get her number. How does she do it?*

Well, she doesn't. *Huh? That's right—she's not really doing anything. She's just being herself, without trying too hard to put on a show. Here are some theories that say you don't have to go out looking for love. If you're putting out the right energy, the boys will come to you.*

HOW TO *NOT* LOOK FOR GUYS LIKE A LAUREN

Lauren's is a pretty successful dater, so you might be surprised to learn that Lauren's philosophy is to *not* go out looking for guys. It's like trying to find four-leaf clovers—the harder you look, the less you find them. It's when you relax and just lie back that the perfect guy (or four-leaf clover) just appears in front of you.

"You meet guys when you're not looking, and when you're not trying," she says. "I think about all those nights that I've spent hours getting ready for a party or tried on five outfits before heading to the club. I never met one guy who ended up being more than a fling.

I've met all my boyfriends when I was least expecting it." Lauren might be having lunch with Audrina somewhere. They're just sitting at an outdoor table, enjoying their chicken salads, talking about whatever happened last night, not even *thinking* about meeting someone, and then they look up and—*bam*—the world's hottest waiter is standing right there. Perfect opportunity!

Girls who seem desperate to meet someone (you probably know a few of those) almost never do. Lauren thinks there's another reason why you shouldn't go out looking for boyfriends: "When you're looking for someone, you're really looking for anyone, and you tend to settle. You find the best available thing, and you choose that."

"You should always be okay being by yourself. When you're not looking, and you're truly cool to be on your own, a guy has to be spectacular for you to put in all the effort of a relationship. You won't waste your time with temporary, mediocre guys."

Lauren met Jason at a *Laguna Beach* photo shoot. It was just supposed to be the cast, standing around and forcing smiles while the photographer took the same shot a hundred times. She was expecting a pretty boring day.

Then in walked Jason. Lauren knew him from

school, but she'd never spent much time with him. She took one look at him and said, "I'm going to go out with that guy." Within a few days they were dating, and within a couple of weeks Lauren had herself a new boyfriend. It all happened fast and was totally unexpected.

A couple of years later, Lauren met another guy in the most unexpected place. "I met Brody Jenner on the same night that he met Kristin Cavallari," Lauren remembers. "Believe me, no part of me was thinking this was a guy I was going to date. But before I knew it, he and Kristin were broken up, and Brody was asking for my phone number."

For Lauren, there is no "best" place to meet guys.

The only time you can expect to meet boys is when you least expect it.

HOW AUDRINA MEETS GUYS WHEN SHE'S NOT MEETING GUYS

Audrina is just not into being schlumpy. After all, as she says, "Every day is a good day to look good."

"My mother taught me that. Sometimes when I spend the night at her house in Orange County, I'll try to sneak out of the house in pajamas the next morning. My mom *always* catches me. She'll say, 'Take a shower! Do something with your hair! Put on something cute!' "

"I tell her that I'm just driving straight home, but she says, 'You never know what will happen. You never know who you'll see.' I guess she thinks I might be pulled over by a cute policeman!" Hey, haven't we all been caught at Starbucks in that big old college T-shirt, gym shorts, and sneakers, hiding under a baseball cap and hoping no one will notice us? And of course, that's the day when Mr. Sexy Biceps, the neighbor across the hall, comes in and stands behind us in line.

So many girls spend way too much money on

clothes, hair, and makeup. So why are they walking around in their sweats, looking as if they haven't showered in the last week? In Audrina's opinion, what you do to go out during the day should be the same as what you do to go out at night—don't spend your days walking around town in flip-flops, wearing the same old tank top you wore yesterday, then spend three hours getting ready to go to dinner.

Audrina wonders, "What are they saving it for? Today is a day of your life when you're young, pretty, and single. That's enough of a reason to get dressed up."

"Whenever I leave my house, I try to look nice. I don't get dressed like I'm going to the Oscars, but if I'm going out into the world, I'll do something with my hair and throw an outfit together."

"Why not? So many of my cute clothes are comfortable, and I'm more comfortable with myself when I look nice. And does it really take any more time to put on a cute pair of jeans than it does to put on those old sweats that make your butt look saggy?"

Audrina is speaking from experience. Once, she was in line at M Café, waiting to buy a muffin. A cute guy was waiting behind her for the same kind of muffin, and he started talking to her. The guy was Shannon Leto, the drummer for 30 Seconds to Mars.

"He was a great guy, we dated for a couple of

months, and we're still friends," Audrina recalls. "Maybe he would have still talked to me if I was wearing sweats and a baseball cap, but I definitely wouldn't have been as comfortable talking to him. The whole time I would have been thinking, 'Why didn't I do my hair this morning? Why didn't I wear something cute?'"

Confidence is key when meeting guys, and nothing helps you feel more confident than looking cute. So dry your hair, put on a little mascara and some lip gloss—it'll only take a few extra minutes in the morning, and who knows? You might wind up sharing a muffin with someone special.

HOW TO WORK THE BACK BURNER LIKE A HEIDI

Some guys are perfectly happy finding a girl in line at the bakery. Some guys, on the other hand, like to know what they're getting into before they commit. So Heidi offers this advice for finding guys: "The best way to get a boyfriend is to have a boyfriend."

What? How can you get a boyfriend when you have a boyfriend? Don't worry, Heidi's not talking about

Lingo Dictionary

● ● ● ● ● ● ● ● ●

*The most important thing in any relationship is communi-
cation, but it's hard to communicate when you're speaking
different languages.*

*Here are some key words, terms, and catchphrases for
expressing yourself in the twenty-first century.*

Baller *n.* A successful and/or wealthy person ("He just had
twenty-twos put on his Escalade—he's a total *baller*")

Beast Out *v.* To overindulge in rich food ("I went to In-N-
Out late night and *beasted out* on double-doubles")

Bovs *adv.* Beyond obvious ("Was I mad when she crashed my
party? *Bovs!*" See also NATCH, OBVS, OBVY, and TOTES)

Butt Hurt *adj.* Deeply upset ("He got all *butt hurt* when I
didn't call him back")

Foxymoron *n.* An attractive, stupid person ("He was doing
everything right . . . until he decided to talk. He's such a
foxymoron")

Ho on the Low *n.* A girl who appears virtuous in public but
behaves badly in private ("She acts like a little princess,
but she's really just a *ho on the low*")

Hobeau *n.* A significant other with bad hygiene ("You'll
smell her boyfriend before you see him. He's a total *hobeau*")

Idiot Shivers *n.* The feeling you experience when someone
else does something so embarrassing that it affects you

("She looked like such a moron on TMZ.com. It gave me the total *idiot shivers*")

Ish *adj.* Suffix meaning "to a certain extent" ("She's smart, funny, and pretty . . . *ish*")

Jump-off *n.* A one-night stand ("I knew this wasn't going to turn into anything long-term. It was just a *jump-off*")

Loc Up *v.* To take immediate action ("He was up in my face, so I had to *loc up*")

Nontourage *n.* A group of hangers-on who shadow a star ("I was psyched he came, but not so psyched he brought his *nontourage*")

Plus One *n.* An uninvited person who tags along with invited guests ("The A-list left early, but the *plus ones* stayed all night")

Sidechick *n.* A mistress ("He's had the same girlfriend for years, but he's creeping around with a *sidechick*")

Slue *n.* A woman of questionable reputation ("She's hooked up with every guy in this club. She's a total *slue*!")

Twelfth of Nevuary *n.* A nonexistent date when something will never happen ("We have to go out sometime. How does the *twelfth of Nevruary* work for you?")

Whole Bowl of Wrong *n.* Something you can't resist, although you know it's bad for you ("He has a reputation, a criminal record, and a girlfriend, but he looked *good*. He was just a *whole bowl of wrong*") cheating or anything. She means that sometimes a guy will check out another guy's girlfriend. Then, when the couple breaks up, he makes his move. After all, when a guy finds out you have a boyfriend, it tells him a lot about you. You're the girl that some guy has given up all other girls to be with. And you must be pretty special for some guy to devote all his time and energy to keeping you happy. You're worth something. You're desired. You're in demand. That's a pretty good first impression.

As much as guys claim to be tough and strong and independent, they do really care what other guys think. As Heidi puts it, "Guys are happy to be with a girl that other guys have signed off on. No matter how cute a girl seems, if she doesn't have a boyfriend, she's a gamble. A guy will always be asking, 'What's wrong with her? Is she high-maintenance? Is she crazy?' A guy would much rather date a girl who's passed those tests than experiment himself." For instance, maybe you've been friends with the same group for a long time—guys and girls. Everyone hangs out together and knows each other really well—*as friends*. But then you hook up with a guy in the group. The two of you start going out. Now, the guys in the group might see you in a different way. They can see how you act toward a boy-friend.

Heidi remembers her dating life before she got serious with Spencer: "A couple of years ago, I was dating a surfer named Bron. I knew he wasn't the guy I was going to spend the rest of my life with, but he was nice and he was fun, so we dated for a little while. When Spencer came along, I wasn't this desperate little girl hoping to bag a boyfriend. I was involved, I was spoken for, and I was more of a challenge. Spencer admits that only made him go after me harder."

"Of course, I upgraded from Bron to Spencer, and now that Spencer is the guy I'm going to spend the rest of my life with, there's nothing left to upgrade. But before I got rid of last year's model, I made sure I had the new and improved version ready and waiting." Wow.

WHO DID WHAT?

1. *Drove back to a guy's house after a date because she didn't get a good-night kiss*
2. *Went on two dates in one day*
3. *Kissed two guys on one New Year's Eve*
4. *Prank-called a "cuddle party"*
5. *Kissed Lauren's ex*
6. *Put her cheating boyfriend on speakerphone . . . in front of the girl he was cheating with*
7. *Wrote love poetry for her ex-boyfriend*
8. *Changed her number to get space from a persistent ex*
9. *Got a tattoo of her boyfriend's initial*
10. *Had designer jewelry made for her boyfriend on his birthday*
11. *Threw a drink on a girl who was messing with her friend*
12. *Picked a fight with a rude football player*
13. *Dressed as Madonna for Halloween*

ANSWER KEY: *1. L; 2. A; 3. W; 4. H; 5. W; 6. H; 7. H; 8. W; 9. L; 10. L; 11. A; 12. H; 13. A*

Heidi definitely knows how to get what she wants. But she's got a point. You wouldn't sell your car until you had a new one picked out, and you wouldn't quit your job until you had a new one lined up. According to Heidi, boyfriends are no different.

Where the Boys Are

When you're looking for love, it can seem as if no matter where you look, you just can't find the boys. Where are they hiding? In some secret central guy basement somewhere, all playing Halo?

Well, trust us, they're not. The guys actually are out there. It's just that sometimes you have to go hunt for them. Luckily for us, our dating experts know the best places to zero in for the kill.

HOW TO HUNT LIKE A HEIDI

The music is pumping, the lights are low, the dance floor is packed. Everyone is dressed up and looking to have a good time. What better place to meet guys than a club? Heidi agrees, "You can't go wrong at a club."

After all, most guys don't go to clubs just to stand around and stare at each other. They want to meet girls, just as girls want to meet them. We hesitate to say "meat market," but, hey, that's not always a *bad* thing, right?

As Heidi says, "Girls have all the power at clubs. We always get right in, while guys always have to wait in line. We usually drink for free, while guys line up to buy us drinks or share their bottle." And girls are *always* outnumbered at clubs. "That's just more boys for me to pick from," Heidi explains. "Every guy I see is a possible dance partner, flirting partner, or maybe something more." This isn't just true for Heidi. When Lauren and Audrina went to Les Deux one night, Lauren started talking to a hot guy from London within just a few minutes. She brought him over to the girls' table and introduced him to Audrina and Whitney. He was a nice guy, it turned out, and any of the three girls could have gone out with him.

Of course, plenty of guys at clubs are interested in one thing and one thing only, and it doesn't take a neuroscientist to figure out what that might be: hook-ups. But Heidi explains, "You meet cheesy guys who want to hook up *everywhere*." So don't avoid clubs, just use your head. If you don't want to meet annoying make-out artists, don't talk to them. Focus on that tall guy standing by the bar, wearing a nice white shirt and looking lonely.

Of course, there's nothing wrong with meeting a guy at the grocery store (actually, the grocery store is an awesome place to meet boys), or at the gym, or at your brother's best friend's cousin's house party. But, as Heidi observes, a guy who's out for the night is "more likely to be dressed nicely, be successful, and have a lot of friends. You know he likes to go out and have fun, and he's not afraid to spend a little money to treat himself—and hopefully you!—well." You can't say that for a guy you meet while picking out brands of mac and cheese.

WHERE WHITNEY *WON'T* MEET A GUY

We're not all Heidis; some of us just don't thrive on the party circuit. For the Whitneys, "A club is not the right place to meet a guy."

According to Whitney, the problem with clubs is

that they can bring out the worst in guys—even sweet ones. It's as if the minute they walk past the velvet rope, they transform into some slick club dude, complete with greased hair and unbuttoned shirt. "I have some really cool guy friends who aren't cheesy at all, but when we go out together, they use these awful pickup lines on girls," Whitney says. "It's just impossible to make a good first impression when a guy is drunk and using stupid lines." Ever heard this one? "Am I dead, Angel? Because this must be heaven." Yeah. That's what she's talking about.

To meet nice, sweet guys, Whitney prefers to let someone else vet her possible picks—she believes the best way to meet guys is to be introduced to them through your friends: "I've been introduced to all my boyfriends by people I already know. My friends know me better than anyone, so they're good judges of whether I'll get along with someone or not. It's so much easier when one of your friends has already signed off on someone."

This is so true. Think of a first date between Whitney and a guy we'll call Ryan. The date does not start off well—he's late picking her up, he's wearing a T-shirt to a nice restaurant, and the conversation is awkward. If Whitney hadn't been introduced to Ryan by Lauren, she might be tempted to end the date early and forget about him. But Lauren swore that he's the world's sweetest guy and treats girls really well. So Whitney grits her teeth and sticks it out through the rest of dinner. And once Ryan loosens up, they have a much easier time talking. He explains that even though he Googled the directions to her apartment, he got a little lost finding the place—that's why he was late. As for the T-shirt, he'd thought the place they were going to was much more casual. He'd never usually wear this, he says. Whitney and Ryan wind up sharing a giant piece of chocolate cake for dessert and having a really good time laughing and talking. If Ryan hadn't been vetted by Lauren first, Whitney would have lost confidence in him and would never have found out what a great guy he is.

Not only is it easier to trust people your friends know, it's easier to talk to them. Most likely you know some of the same people, like to do some of the same things— you might even have gone to the same elementary school, who knows? All potential conversation starters.

You shouldn't worry that meeting people through

your friends means limiting yourself to a small group. If you have thirty trusted friends, and they each have thirty trusted friends of their own, that's nine hundred people right there. You'll be eighty years old before you go on dates with nine hundred guys! And as Whitney explains, "You spend so much of your life surrounded by friends. Weddings, birthday parties, and graduations are all events where *every* guest is a friend of a friend."

Audrina's Bad-Date Timeline

8:00   Danny picks Audrina up. He looks as if he spent more time on his hair than she did on hers.
      Bad sign.

8:15   Remembering an earlier conversation, Audrina asks Danny about his day at the beach. He replies, "Did I say I was going to the beach? I must have lied."
      This is going to be a long night.

8:30   Out of nowhere, Danny starts a story about some random girl's breast implants. The story seems to have no point, and no end.

8:40   Still talking about boobs.

9:00   Danny stops the conversation to check his
        messages. He says it's his agent, then looks
        to see if Audrina's impressed.
            She's not.

9:10   Audrina asks Danny how long it's been since
        his last long-term relationship. He replies,
        "I haven't had a long-term relationship,
        probably ever."
            Audrina is beginning to see why.

9:30   Heidi calls Audrina. They've worked out a
        code, so that if Danny is really cute and
        sweet, Audrina is supposed to tell Heidi that
        the food is great.
            Audrina tells Heidi that the food is
        "greasy." She's actually talking about both
        her date *and* her food.

9:50   Danny puts the whole salad on the end of his
        fork, then takes tiny bites, as if he were eat-
        ing an ice cream cone.
            The date can't get any worse.

9:55   Danny declares, "This salad's like a party!"
            The date just got worse.

· · ·

So don't worry if you haven't met your dream guy yet—one of your friends may already have met him for you!

HOW AUDRINA MEETS MEN

Maybe you're someone who isn't just all about work and friends, friends and work. Someone like Audrina has a lot of other interests too—such as music. So Audrina advises, "You meet the best people doing what you love."

"I've always loved going to rock shows. I love live music, and I love musicians. Lucky for me, I can find them both in one place." Rock shows—and any other kind of music show or art show or bookstore readings—can be fantastic places to meet guys. For one thing, you always have a ready-made conversation starter. Picture this scenario: You're at a show, wearing your band T-shirt, cute jeans, and your vintage motorcycle boots. You see a cute guy rocking out to the music, just enjoying himself, and maneuver over so that you're standing next to him.

You (watching the band but also watching him): "Isn't this an awesome show?"

Him (stops dancing and turns to look at the goddess standing next to him—you!): "Yeah, I love these guys."

You: "Did you see them in L.A. this summer?"

Him: "No, I heard that show was amazing. Did you see them?"

You (feeling really, really glad you read the review of the L.A. show in *Rolling Stone*): "No, but I heard they played 'Simon's Addiction.'"

Him: "No way!"

Okay, you get the idea. If you weren't at a concert, you might have to search around a little harder for conversation.

A lot of Audrina's friends go to clubs every night. As we heard from Heidi, clubs can be great places to meet guys. But for the alternative girl, they might just not be the right *kind* of guy. As Audrina explains, "Clubs are filled with guys, but it's rare that you meet boyfriend material at clubs. All you meet at the club are *mactors,* our word for model/actors. There's nothing wrong with mactors, but when you've spent enough time in a club, you see that it's the same mactors, night after night. The club scene in L.A. seems big at first, but it gets small fast. Pretty soon, all the mactors have hooked up with all your girlfriends. It's not a place to find a serious guy."

"Clubs are also filled with older businessmen.

THE HILLS

There's nothing wrong with that, except sometimes it seems like they're not really there to have a good time. They're really only there to try to pick up young girls." If you're interested in more than just a hookup, don't waste your time on these guys.

For Audrina, the best place to meet guys is at live-music venues, "because everyone there loves live music as much as I do. It's not just that I love artsy musicians and rocker types with tattoos—which I do. It's just that I love meeting guys that I have something in common with and guys who are passionate about something."

It's a simple rule, but a good one: you meet the best guys doing the things you love best.

Making the First Move

. . . .

We've all encountered that guy who just doesn't seem to get it. He seems to like you, but he still hasn't asked you out, despite all of your best methods: sparkling conversation, gentle flirtation, delicate hints. So what's his deal? Is he shy or just plain stupid?

Either is possible. A lot of guys are shy—they can be just as self-conscious and insecure as girls. He might think

38

you're out of his league. Or maybe he's afraid of being rejected. Or—and this is true for even the best of men—he might just be oblivious. So many smart, nice, funny guys are completely clueless when it comes to the "Hey, ask me out!" hints you've been dropping for the last week. He might still think the two of you are "just friends." How do you let him know you're ready for more?

Asking a guy out is one of the trickiest, most potentially ego-wounding situations in dating. Audrina, Whitney, Lauren, and Heidi have had a lot of experience making the first move. Being timid takes too long. Here's how you know when it's time to take action.

HOW TO BREAK THE ICE LIKE AN AUDRINA

Sometimes, you're going to have to make a decision: either make the first move, and risk rejection, or let a potentially cool guy slip away. Audrina usually goes for the first option. "If a guy is moving too slowly," says Audrina, "I'm not afraid to make the first move."

Naturally, we all wish hot guys would just run up to us on the street every day and beg for our phone numbers. But it doesn't usually work that way, which is why Audrina takes matters into her own hands: "Sometimes, a guy will *want* to go out with you, but something is holding him back. When it's clear that the guy isn't going to make the first move, you can either sit back and wait forever, or you can take control of the situation. I choose to take control."

"Once, I was having lunch with some girlfriends down in the O.C. We were at this outdoor restaurant on Main Street in Huntington, and a group of cute guys kept looking over at us. It was pretty obvious that they wanted to talk to us, but none of them got up the nerve to come and say hi."

"They wouldn't make the first move, so I did. I said, 'Hey, are you guys going to come over? Are you ever going to talk to us?' The guys came over right away. Once I broke the ice, they were totally comfortable, and they turned out to be totally nice."

What started out as a normal day ended up turning into a casual group date for Audrina and her friends: "We hung out for the rest of the day, going from restaurant to restaurant and bar to bar. Nothing serious ended up happening, but a fun date got more fun because we had some cute guys to share it with. If I hadn't said anything, they sure never would have. We'd still be thinking about the cute, shy boys from the O.C."

Of course, there's always the chance that the guy

isn't asking you out because he's not interested. Or he has a girlfriend. Or a boyfriend (oops). Or he's really attached to his dog. Or he just broke up with someone and doesn't want a relationship. All of these things are potentially embarrassing. No one's saying rejection is fun. But, hey, you're a strong woman, right? So don't worry about a little rejection—it happens to everyone. Literally everyone. As Audrina says, "If you don't make the move, you'll always be asking yourself, 'What if?' I'd rather make the first move, take control, and take a chance."

CAN A WHITNEY MAKE THE FIRST MOVE?

All right, you might be saying. Asking a guy out is great if you're an Audrina—the gutsy, bold, risk-taking type. But what about the Whitneys? It can be really hard to ask someone out if you're shy yourself. "I haven't done it yet," Whitney says, "but one day, I will ask a guy out."

"I just haven't gotten around to it, although I've always said that I would. When I see a cute guy, I wish I could just go talk to him or buy him a drink. I haven't worked up the nerve to do it yet, but one of these days, I will." That's easier said than done. Have you ever been in this situation? You're at a club with your friends, and one of your friends spots a cute guy standing at the bar. You look at him and he stares back at you. He smiles but doesn't come over. All of your friends agree that you should go up and talk to him, maybe have a drink with him. Slowly, you get up and make your way over to the bar. You stand next to the cute guy and stare straight ahead, pretending you're looking for the bartender. He smiles at you and says, "Hi." Your heart is pounding but you manage to smile back—then you flee, back to your table of friends.

It's hard to take the risk of asking someone out! How would you like to be a guy? Then you'd have to do it all the time. Whitney can sympathize with this: "Guys have to go through so much in dating. Think about it. Most guys will ask out one hundred percent of the women they go out with in their lifetime. That's a lot of pressure, and there's no reason girls can't take a little of that pressure off of them."

"One of these days, I'm going to get up the guts

and make the first move," Whitney vows. "I'm going to march straight up to a guy and ask him out. I don't think there's any reason why a girl can't ask a guy out—although I have a feeling my mom would disagree!"

Top Five Underrated Places to Meet Guys

1. **The grocery store:** Excellent opportunities for conversation starters, plus you can ask for his help getting the cereal down from that high top shelf.

2. **The car wash:** There's nothing guys like to do more than talk about their cars. So while you're sitting in that stuffy little room, bored out of your mind, check out who else might be waiting for a touchless gleaming hot-wax treatment.

3. **The farmers' market:** Who doesn't like cute crunchy guys with dirt under their nails? Ask the hottie who just sold you some organic arugula how to cook it. You never know—he might offer to show you himself.

4. **The dog park:** Even if you don't have a dog, you can always borrow one for an hour. Check out the outdoorsy type throwing a Frisbee for his Lab.

5. **The bookstore:** Ask him if he's read the new Harry Potter, then offer to give him a summary over coffee in the café.

3

GET IN TOUCH

Can I Call?

• •

Sunday night, 10 p.m. You're at home, staring at your cell phone, which is sitting on your bedside table like some little sleeping animal. You've done it—you've finally met a really sweet, nice, funny, cute guy at your friend's house party on Friday night, and you guys talked for hours. You were flirtatious, but not over the top, and the two of you found out that you actually had a lot in common. As the party was winding down, the two of you finally pried your-

selves off the couch, and he did the deed—he asked for your number and said, "Cool. I'll call you this weekend." Okay. This weekend. Saturday—no call. Saturday night—no. Sunday—nada. Now it's Sunday night and your phone has never been quieter. You pick it up and press TALK just to make sure it's still working. It is. You call one of your friends and say, "Call me right back." She does—the phone rings. Okay, it's not the phone. Maybe he's trapped under something heavy. Maybe his phone fell in the toilet. But that still doesn't answer the question of the night: are you going to call him? You don't want to look desperate. But on the other hand, what are you waiting for? Prince Charming to sweep you off your feet? Why can't you do a little reverse sweeping for a change?

Here are the factors you need to consider before dialing those magic numbers.

WHY AUDRINA'S NOT AFRAID TO CALL BOYS

The take-charge types among us, such as Audrina, think that it's time for girls to take more control of the situation. Who made the rule that guys have to do the

calling? And besides, aren't rules made to be broken?
"If I want to talk to a guy, I'll call that guy," Audrina
says.

"Some girls say that I should always let the guy call
me, because if a guy doesn't call right away, it means
he's not into me," says Audrina, but the same isn't always true of her. "I know that sometimes I'm dying to
talk to someone, but I get so busy, I literally don't have
a chance to pick up the phone. So how come if a guy
doesn't call you every five minutes, you're supposed to
assume he's over you? That's really negative, and I
don't want to think that way."

Audrina broke the Do Not Call rule over and over

with one boy in particular—Justin Bobby: "When I was dating Justin, he would disappear for days at a time. No messages, no e-mails, no texts—just silence. This was partly because he loved to surprise me. He wouldn't call for a week, then I'd be out one night, and he'd send me a text with exactly what I was wearing. While I was trying to figure out how he knew what I had on, I'd look up, and he'd be across the club. Sometimes, he wouldn't even text me until the next day. He'd write me a message about where I was, what I was wearing, and who I was talking to."

"Sometimes, I couldn't wait for the surprises, so I would call him. I had to. If I never called him, I never would have spoken to him. I'd give him a hard time about not calling me, which he didn't always like, but I had to let him know how I felt."

Audrina figures that whether the guy is interested or not, it's better to know. At least then you can figure out your next move—even if it means moving on: "I say, 'You'll never know if you don't call a guy.' Hopefully, he's into you, and he'll be happy to hear your voice. If he's not into you, there's nothing you can do, but at least you'll make him tell it to you straight."

HEIDI'S TELEPHONE PHILOSOPHY

Audrina is never one to hold back. Heidi, on the other hand, likes to play things a little more carefully. A phone conversation is like a diplomatic negotiation—you have to tread lightly. "You have nothing to lose by calling a guy," Heidi says, "but you don't have much to gain."

Think about it, Heidi says. "When a guy doesn't call you, and you don't call the guy, you don't get the guy. When a guy doesn't call you, and you *do* call the guy, you might just get the guy. It's a slim chance, but

there is a chance, and at least you're taking control of the situation."

"Girls will say that they have too much pride to call a guy. These are the same girls who check their Black-Berry every ten seconds and can't carry on a conversation with you because they're always looking at their phones, hoping he'll call. And you're going to tell me that you have pride? Really?"

If you do take the risk and get the guy on the phone, Heidi has some valuable advice: "Some guys may like it when you call, but no guy likes it when you call about *calling*. Never say things like 'Wow, I haven't heard from you in so long' or 'I thought you lost my number.' Guys can't stand it when you lecture them, and the nagging just makes you seem like you've been obsessing over him. That's probably why the guy didn't call you in the first place." News flash: guys are really, really not into obsessive, clingy girls. There's nothing wrong with being assertive. Just don't turn into a stalker.

Heidi's advice: keep calls casual and fun: "It's okay to call with a funny story, or because something made you think of him. That tells the guy that you're laid-back, and you're not trying to force him into a serious committed relationship. You're just calling because the mood struck you, and he should feel free to do the same." If you do it right, the guy may never even realize you're calling because he never called you. He'll be too occupied listening to your charming self.

For instance, Heidi might be out somewhere with her friends. She's been waiting for a guy named Trent to call for a week now, and he's still MIA. So, she works some magic: She calls Trent, and when he answers, she says, "Hey, it's Heidi. We're all out at this Brazilian steak house."

"Hey," Trent says. "What's up?"

"Not much. But we're sitting here in front of these giant piles of meat and they keep bringing more over. It's hilarious."

"I've never been to that place," Trent says.

"I thought you were a huge carnivore!"

"I am. Maybe I should check it out."

Heidi can smell victory ahead. "Well, why don't you come over? We'll be here forever."

"Yeah, okay." Trent sounds perked up at the thought of consuming huge amounts of meat.

So if Heidi hadn't taken the plunge and just called Trent, they might not even have gotten together. But even though he hadn't called in a week, she never mentioned that on the phone. She just told him that she was having a good time somewhere, doing something she knew he liked, and invited him out.

THE HILLS

So if you're feeling bold, and you want to take a chance on calling a guy, remember to keep it light. Call about something funny, call about something fun, but just don't call him about *not* calling you.

WHY WHITNEY NEVER CALLS BOYS

"To call or not to call, that is the question." Unlike Hamlet, Whitney doesn't spend a lot of time on this issue: this girl's phone takes incoming calls only. "It's a bad idea to call guys. Period."

"I hate to be harsh," Whitney says, "but girls need to understand: when a guy doesn't call you, it's because he doesn't like you. If a guy likes you, he calls you. It's pretty much that simple."

For any boys out there who might be reading this, take note now: Whitney does not buy the "But I was too busy to call!" excuse: "There's no way you can tell me that a guy can't find two minutes a day to call a girl he's got a crush on. You have to take that as a message. He's telling you there are more important things in his life than you, and that's fine, because you don't want that anyway. You want to find someone who wants to give you two hours a day." Sorry, boys. The Whitneys among us demand the best from their men. If you can't treat her right—hint: call her!—she's not going to be interested.

And another thing about the Whitneys—they don't play games. "If a guy doesn't call when he says he's going to, or if a guy makes me wait, I have to think long and hard about whether I'm going to speak with him again. I don't like games, and I don't like feeling silly. A guy who can't keep the commitment of a five-minute phone call is probably not a guy I'm going to work hard to build a relationship with. Besides, it sends a really bad message—if you'll accept bad treatment from a guy and still come back for more, what else will you put up with?"

When it comes to calling, Whitney's rule is pretty straightforward: "If a boy likes you, he calls. If a boy doesn't like you, he doesn't. So if you're the one calling a boy, you're calling a boy who doesn't like you."

The Point of No Return

Okay, you tell yourself on that Sunday night at 10 p.m. He's not going to call. That's it. You brush your teeth, put on some old boxers and a T-shirt, and resign yourself to a night spent with the thrilling company of your American-history textbook. Then, just as you climb into bed, it happens. The phone rings. You lunge across the bed, grab the phone like a lifeline, and—

Stop! Don't answer the phone. "Huh?" You might say. "Why not?" You've been waiting for him to call, and he's called. So what's the problem?

Well, Lauren believes calling a guy back can be a big mistake. It may seem illogical, but if you like the guy who's calling you, she thinks you might want to ease off and just take a breather for a minute.

Here's Lauren's explanation of her No Return Policy.

HOW TO BLOW OFF THE FIRST CALL LIKE A LAUREN

"You never want to seem too available," Lauren explains, "so as a rule, I never return first phone calls."

"When you call a guy right back, you can come off as a little eager," Lauren says. "But when you don't respond to the first call, you let the guy know that you have something going on in your life. You're not sitting around waiting for guys to call." Or sitting

at home on Sunday night doing American-history homework.

Although this may sound dishonest, Lauren insists that it's not a trick: "I hear all this advice on how to seem like you're really busy, appear like you have a lot going on, or pretend like you have a life. Well, I actually *do* have a life, so I don't have to pretend. Not calling back right away just lets the guy know how busy I actually am." Of course, if you don't happen to be superbusy when the guy calls, there's nothing wrong with a little harmless deception. After all, *he* doesn't know what you're doing, right?

"If a guy calls me a second time," Lauren explains,

"then I know that he is secure and persistent enough to keep up with me. You need a guy who hits that right balance—a guy who has some confidence and persistence, but not too much. There's a difference between being interested and being a stalker." Lauren's method puts the power back in your hands. Now you get to decide whether he's going to be worth your time—and worth answering that second call.

"So if I don't return a guy's first call, that doesn't mean I'm not interested," Lauren says. "I'm just testing how interested the guy is. But if I don't return the guy's second call, then he's pretty much done."

Giving Up the Digits

· ·

It's another Saturday night out. The guy has a piece of chili cheese fry in his front teeth, and from his breath you can confirm that chili cheese fry order definitely came with onions. He's been talking about his love for hunting for the last hour without taking a breath, and now all you can think of are all the baby animals he's probably shot dead.

This is really not going to work. Unfortunately, Mr. Chili Cheese Fry doesn't quite get it. In fact, he thinks the

two of you, as he puts it, "really have like a psychic con-
nection, you know what I mean?" Uh, yeah.

You manage to telegraph a frantic "Rescue me" eye-
brow raise to your friends, who rush over and tell you that
you're all totally late and you have go right now, this min-
ute. You grab your bag, and then the moment happens. He
leans over and, with a fresh blast of onion breath in your
face, asks for your number.

How do you avoid giving out personal information to
people you'd prefer not to get personal with?

HOW TO HOLD BACK
LIKE A WHITNEY

You can give all the excuses in the world, but if you're a
Whitney, you're going to have to go with the nice-girl
approach: be honest. As Whitney herself puts it, "Just
say no . . . thank you."

Mr. Chili Cheese Fry might need to work on his
conversation topics, but he's still a person, and much
as we might hate to admit it, he has feelings and an ego
just like the rest of us. So it's time for a little Golden
Rule action—avoid the games. Whitney offers this ad-

vice: "When a guy asks me for my number and I'm one hundred percent sure that I'm not interested, I'll just politely refuse to give it to him. I'm a big believer in honesty, and I find that the straightforward approach is the best. How are you going to be honest with a guy you like if you can't even be honest with the guys you're never going to see again?"

Okay, you say, thanks for the lecture on honesty, but really, isn't it sometimes better to give the guy the number to the local pizza place? "A lot of girls think it's easier to give out a fake number," explains Whitney, "but that only gives the guy false hope. I imagine him rushing to call right away, then being disappointed when he realized I lied."

"The guy was only being nice by showing interest and asking for the number, so I don't want to embarrass him. I'd rather give him a minor letdown tonight than a major disappointment in a day or two. And if the guy isn't nice and is sort of annoying, I feel even more compelled not to give a fake number. It's not fair to have him calling and hassling someone else."

Whitney believes that honesty brings you good dating karma—and that lying can come back to haunt you. "Hollywood is a small town," Whitney says, "and this can be a small world. You're not going to like every guy who likes you, but there's absolutely no reason to make a guy who started out liking you end up hating you." You never know when you're going to run into that guy at Whole Foods—accompanied by the cutest granola-crunchy guy you've ever seen. Now, do you want him telling his hot friend how he dialed Jay's Auto Repair thinking it was your cell he was calling?

Honesty is always the best policy. Tell him that you're flattered, tell him that you appreciated it, but tell him that you just can't tell him your number.

Pulling In the Digits

* *

Of course, it's a rough world out there. So we understand why some girls just prefer to keep it close to home and only give out their numbers to a select few. Or to no one at all. Or to keep Jay's Auto Repair at the top of their phone address book so they can give it out to any and all requests for digits.

But leave it to ever-resourceful Audrina to think of another way. You can decide when and if you ever talk to the guy. Even if you're not into him tonight, you can still tuck him away in a little glass box labeled IN CASE OF EMERGENCY. You never know how you might feel tomorrow.

HOW TO BEAT THE NUMBERS GAME LIKE AN AUDRINA

None of our dating experts like to lie, but not everyone believes in brutal honesty like Whitney. Audrina has a good ego-smoothing trick for dealing with awkward phone-number requests: "If I don't feel like giving a guy my number, I just get his instead."

"Some girls think it's bad to ask for a guy's number, but I have never had a problem with it. If I'm talking to a guy that I'm not interested in and he asks for my number, I don't want to ruin his night by saying I would never go out with him. No one likes to let someone down, so asking for his number is better for both of us."

Once again, the power is back in your hands. If you've got his number, then you get to call the shots. Not only do you decide *if* you're going to call him, you also decide *when*. "There are times when I'm talking to a good guy but I'm seeing someone else, or I'm getting over a breakup, or it's just not the right time to give out my number. Rather than say no and end any chance to get to know the guy in the future, I ask for the guy's number instead. When you do the asking, a lot of hard situations become easy."

Picture this sample conversation between a guy named Charlie and Audrina. They've been chatting at a coffee shop for a while, and Audrina starts gathering her stuff to leave.

Audrina: "This was fun, but I've got to go. My friends are waiting for me."

Charlie (starts looking nervous): "Okay, yeah. Um . . ." He loses his nerve.

Audrina waits patiently. She's been through this a million times.

Charlie: "So, can I call you to hang out sometime?" His face is scarlet.

Audrina (makes sure to wait a moment. She's already decided she doesn't want to give Charlie her number, but she doesn't want it to be too obvious): "Actually, can I get your number? I'm really busy these days so it might be easier if I just call you sometime."

Audrina pulls out her phone and taps in Charlie's number, and everyone leaves happy. Charlie's feelings are preserved, and Audrina's got a potential nice guy on tap—and the ball in her court, which is the way she likes it.

Audrina also is not a fan of giving out phony phone numbers: "I don't like lying. If a guy is nice enough to say that he's interested and ask me out, I don't want to make him feel stupid later. Plus, you don't want to walk into a club filled with guys who are all mad because you tricked them. Instead, I'll just say, 'I don't really give out my number, but why don't you give me yours?' There are no hurt feelings, and I don't have to lie."

The trick is good for getting out of potentially awkward situations, but Audrina has also used this strategy to put boys "on hold." You know how it's nice to have a reserve stash of junk food hidden somewhere in your room or your kitchen, ready for when the M&M's craving hits at three in the morning? The same thing is true of guys. Audrina says, "If the guy seems nice, sometimes I really will call him later. I was dating someone else when I met Justin, and I told him that I never hang out with more than one guy at once. I wouldn't give him my number, but I took his instead. Justin probably thought I was blowing him off, but when I broke up with the guy I'd been seeing, I gave him a call to see if he wanted to meet up. We never would have started hanging out seriously if I had given him a fake number or just told him no."

By getting a guy's number you can save the guy's

feelings . . . and you can build up a nice "reserve stash" also.

Subtext

• •

Ah, the intoxicating sound of that little bee-doop *and the envelope icon appearing on your cell screen. Your guy has sent you another text. You grab your phone, ready for whatever sweet nothings he's written because he so obviously can't keep you off his mind. You press* READ *and . . .*
S up? What r u doing?

That's *your sweet nothing?!*

Well, no one ever said texting was romantic. After all, you're typing on a tiny keypad on a phone for godsakes. It's not exactly Shakespeare writing with a quill by candlelight.

Texting is great for a lot of things, of course—making plans, talking to people in noisy places, sending messages when you're out of cell range, but some think that for love messages, texting is not ideal.

Lauren's "Five Things Every Guy Can Get Right"

1. **It's always nice to give compliments.**
"You don't have to overdo it, but when a girl is going on a first date, you should tell her she looks nice. She put a lot of time and effort into her appearance, so the least you can do is notice."

2. **Watch your manners—with everyone.**
"Every guy is polite towards you on a date. What I look for is how he treats others. I don't want a guy who pretends to be nice to me, but talks down to the valet. A true gentleman who is sure of himself will treat everyone he comes across with dignity and respect."

3. **Don't make a girl work too hard.**
"Girls like to talk about themselves, but not all night. A date is not a job interview. I want to hear things about him too. A lot of times, I have to talk about myself all day. When I go out, I want a chance to sit and listen."

4. **Don't just listen to me—remember me.**
"I like when I know a guy pays attention to

what I've said. When he brings up something I've said before, I know he cares about
what I say."

"Once, in high school, a guy I had just
started dating kidnapped me and took me to
the beach. He had set up a little table, and
he had each of my favorite flowers, foods,
and drinks. It was really one of the sweetest
things I've ever seen. I liked it, because it
showed me he wasn't just nodding along and
smiling when we talked. He cared about
what I said enough to remember it for later."

5. **Make me remember you.**
"I like guys who do things a little bit differently. Do something that makes you stand
out. Dates are repetitive. I've been to restau-
rants before, so if you just pick me up and
take me to dinner, it's going to be hard to
make that evening stand out. Take me somewhere fun that I wouldn't expect."

"Or maybe buy a funny souvenir. It
doesn't have to be expensive, and it
shouldn't be. It should just be something
that I can put on my dresser for a few days
and laugh. Every time I look at it, I'll think of
our fun date and think of you."

WHITNEY'S TEXTING WOES

Whitney believes that traditional is always better, and that texting has got to stop.

"There's no such thing as romantic texting!" she says. "Texting is so impersonal. No matter how much charisma you have in person, none of it comes through in three or four lines of text, so everyone ends up sounding the same. 'S'up? What R U doing? TTYL.' That's not exactly the kind of communication I want to build a serious relationship on." The point of dating someone is to get to know them, of course. It's hard to do that when your conversation is reduced to a bunch of electronic abbreviations.

It's not as if Whitney wants a volume of personally penned love poetry—she just wants a conversation: "I'm not expecting guys to sit down and write me poetry, but I need a little more than three misspelled words on my cell phone screen. Texting might be okay to pass a little information to your friends, or to reach someone in a noisy bar or concert, but for dating, texting is never the right move."

Whitney thinks that sending a text instead of calling is just cowardly. "It's like he couldn't get up the nerve to speak to you live. It also tells you he probably doesn't have a lot to say. If he can fit all his thoughts onto a two-inch screen, that's a bad sign." Right. You know those guys who sit across from you on a date and say about five words all night? This is the electronic equivalent.

Plus, Whitney thinks it's really cute when a guy does get up the nerve to call—it shows that he's willing to put himself out there a little, even if he feels stupid doing it. "There's just something about hearing a guy's voice on the other end of the phone that I really like. Even if he sounds nervous, I don't hold it against him. At least he had the courage and the class to speak with me directly."

In other words, guys, if you can't be bothered to call, don't bother to text.

AUDRINA'S TEXTUAL ATTRACTION

In case you haven't figured it out by now, Whitney and Audrina tend to be total opposites when it comes to guys. So it's not too surprising that Audrina has a totally different opinion of texting and guys than her friend: "I love it."

"I actually prefer getting texts rather than phone calls," says Audrina. "It's easier, it's faster, and I can plan what I'm going to say." It's the same reason people like e-mail and IM—even for romance. Somehow, it's easier to write things than it is to say them.

"I'll write things in a text that I would never say on the phone. After a date, I'll say something like 'Thanks. I had a great time.' I probably wouldn't call him on the phone just to tell him that, but I want him to know. Texting is perfect for that situation."

"I'll also tell guys things that are too difficult to say in a conversation. With a text, I can be more open and more direct. I've told guys I really liked them over text, and I've also told guys to back off. It takes a lot of the pressure off not having a guy on the other end." No awkward pauses, no wondering if your tone sounds too harsh, no having to look a guy in the face as you tell him you don't want to see him anymore.

This is why we need more than one dating guide— both Whitney and Audrina give really good reasons for and against texting. Now it's up to you to choose the situation. If you're breaking up with a sweet guy, do him a favor—don't do it with a text. Have a little decency for his poor guy-ego, and do it in person. But to send a flirtatious little note after a first date, telling him what fun you had—go for it.

Textual Relations

• • • • • • • •

IiDR who the first person was to use an abbreviation in a text instead of the whole word? IMNSHO, that person was a genius. Sure, it may not be grammatically correct, but DILLIGAD? CMIIW, but speed and ease are the name of the game when reading and writing texts.

BSF, if you don't know WTF I'm talking about, you need to study the text dictionary below. Whether it's UR BF, GF, BBF, or FWB, you need to be able to express yourself via text, so LILILI.

TWIWI?

TTFN!

Text and IM Dictionary

2BZ4UQT	Too Busy For You, Cutie
911!	Help!
AWGTHTGTTA?	Are We Going To Have To Go Through This Again?
BFD	Big Frickin' Deal
BRB	Be Right Back
BSF	But Seriously, Folks
BTHOOM	Beats The Hell Out Of Me
BTWBO	Be There With Bells On
CMIIW	Correct Me If I'm Wrong
CSG	Chuckle, Snicker, Grin
DGT	Don't Go There
DILLIGAD?	Do I Look Like I Give A Damn?
DWPKOTL	Deep Wet Passionate Kiss On The Lips
FWB	Friends With Benefits
HBASTD	Hitting Bottom And Starting To Dig
I1DR	I Wonder
IASAP4U	I Always Say A Prayer For You
IKYABWAI?	I Know You Are, But What Am I?
IM2BZ2P	I Am Too Busy To Pee
IMNSHO	In My Not So Humble Opinion
LILILI	Learn It, Love It, Live It
LMAO	Laughing My Ass Off
LYLAS	Love You Like A Sister

NE1^4AD8?	Anyone Up For A Date?
OMDB	Over My Dead Body
OMIK	Open Mouth, Insert Keyboard
OTFL	On The Floor Laughing
OTOH	On The Other Hand
OTOOH	On The Other Other Hand
OTTH	On The Third Hand
PMIGBOM	Put Mind In Gear Before Opening Mouth
PMPL	Peeing My Pants Laughing
SNAFU	Situation Normal: All Effed Up
SSDD	Same Stuff, Different Day
SWAKBALWS	Sealed With A Kiss Because a Lick Won't Stick
TISNC	That Is So Not Cool
TMI	Too Much Information
TTFN	Ta Ta For Now
TTTHTFAL	Talk To The Hand, The Face Ain't Listening
TWIWI?	That Was Interesting, Wasn't It?
WDALYIC?	Who Died And Left You In Charge?
WTF?	WTF?

● ● ●

Friends Don't Let Friends Drink and Dial

• •

You've been thinking about him all weekend. The phone has never been more silent, but you're determined—you're not going to call. If you call him now, he'll know you haven't stopped thinking about him for one second.

To take your mind off not calling, you go out with a few friends. But after a drink or two, a funny thing happens. Your fingers start pulling your phone out of your bag.

No! you tell your fingers. Stop! What are you doing?

Your fingers don't listen—in fact, they're already busily pressing buttons, trying to find his phone number.

You try again to convince your fingers: Stop! This is a terrible mistake! Don't call!

They've found the number.

No! I'll do anything—I'll buy you a really big cocktail ring—just don't call!

But it's no use. Your fingers have pressed his number. It's happened—you have officially drunk-dialed. This is going to be a call you will regret.

Until cell phone companies start installing Breathalyzers, you'll have to police yourself. Here's an argument for why you should never, ever, dial under the influence.

WHY WHITNEY WON'T DRUNK-DIAL

Whitney's rule for drunk-dialing is simple: "If calling sober is a mistake, then calling drunk is a disaster."

"I've seen some of my best friends fall into this trap," Whitney explains. "They've been seeing a guy they like for a little while, but he stopped calling them. My friend will promise not to let it ruin her evening. She says she's not going to think about him, not going to accept any calls from him, and she's definitely not going to call him. Then, a few drinks later, she has her phone out and she's tapping away."

What if you just had a fight with some guy? You've argued, you've broken up, you're not going to see him again. Then the booze hits and it's like someone whiteouted your brain. All of a sudden, you're on the phone, opening the argument back up, telling him what a jerk he is all over again.

Whitney tries to avoid making this mistake at all costs: "Personally, I never drunk-dial. I just don't like feeling vulnerable. If a guy isn't calling you, it's a mistake to call him in the first place, so it's a bigger mistake to call him at the end of the night. If you're drunk enough to make those two mistakes, then you are definitely too drunk to talk with a boy that you like."

Some girls make the mistake of thinking that they're actually *better* when they drink—more relaxed, less inhibited, funnier. Well, anyone who's spent an evening holding up a trashed friend while she tries to claw every guy around her can tell you that booze doesn't exactly bring out the lady in any of us.

Whitney has news for girls who prefer to talk to guys after a few drinks: "They're wrong. A person who has nothing to say when they're sober is only going to be worse when they've been drinking. If you don't believe it, look through your outbox the morning after a big night and read through a few of the texts you wrote. You'll see what I mean."

Whitney tries to stop her friends whenever she sees them making this mistake, but it's hard to reason with someone once she's made up her mind— especially if she's sloshed, so Whitney has had to resort to guerrilla tactics: "Now, I just take their phones away from them. I'll put it in my pocket or hide it in my purse. No matter how much they beg or plead, it doesn't matter. They're not getting it back on my watch. They may be a little annoyed that night, but they *always* thank me in the morning."

Audrina's Texting Catastrophe

Audrina is fun, funny, and adventurous, but sometimes her self-control fails her. "Drunk-dialing is a no-no," Audrina says, "but it's a no-no that I've definitely done. When I have a drink, I get really sensitive, and I don't make good decisions. I don't look at the whole picture, I just do things without thinking. Before you know it, the cell phone comes out." She should probably hand her phone over to someone else before she starts drinking—like giving your friend your car keys.

You'd think that drunken phone calls would be just about the most embarrassing thing ever. But you'd be wrong. Audrina should know: "I used to think there

Asking Guys Out:
A Few Handy Dos and Don'ts

- **Do** keep it casual. This isn't a marriage proposal, and most guys will appreciate the laid-back approach. Just a simple "Do you want to hang out sometime?" will do the job fine.

- **Do** smile and be friendly. If you're nervous, you can easily come across as abrupt or serious, especially if someone doesn't know you. So plaster a somewhat realistic smile on your lips, even if your mouth is so dry you need a cough drop.

- **Don't** think about it too long. If you're going to do something really gutsy, such as leave the hot waiter your number on the check, then do it without making your friends listen to an hour of debating "should I or shouldn't I?"

- **Don't** bring a giant group of giggling friends over with you when you approach a guy. You and he will feel much more comfortable without an audience.

- On the other hand, **don't** worry if he's standing with *his* friends. If the club or party or wherever is noisy, they probably won't be listening to you anyway. And if they are, just fake all the confidence in the world. They'll probably be impressed by your gutsiness.

- **Don't** get too specific. You don't need to ask him if he wants to go get dinner at that new Mexican restaurant next Friday at seven. Just getting his number will do for the first encounter. Then, when you talk on the phone, he might even suggest a place to go.

- **Don't** take it personally if for some reason he refuses. Everyone gets rejected at some point. Just flash him a "your loss" smile and get out of there politely but quickly.

• • •

was nothing more embarrassing than drunk-dialing, until I discovered drunk-texting. Those are worse, because there's a record of it when you wake up. I've gone to my outbox in the morning and discovered whole paragraphs of texts that I don't ever remember writing. And not just harmless, friendly texts—

embarrassing, emotional stuff. Let's just say, it was not pretty."

Audrina remembers a time when she was dating Justin, and she met up with some of his friends at a club. One of them started hitting on her, and it made her upset: "I should have just gone home, let it go, and dealt with it in the morning when everyone had a clear head. Instead, I sent Justin a text saying, 'This guy is supposed to be your friend, but he's here hitting on me behind your back.' Then, the night went on, and I forgot all about it."

But while Audrina was sleeping, Justin read the message and sent an angry text to his friend, who then sent an even angrier text to Audrina. "It was just one little message that I should never have sent in the first place," says Audrina, "but by the time I woke up, it had started a whole chain reaction. Everyone was mad at everyone. It took a whole day for everybody to call each other, explain their side of the story, and apologize."

Obviously, drunk-dialing is a bad idea. But it's like going to the gym: you know you should do it, you know you'll feel better if you do, but sometimes . . . you just don't. Audrina would be the first to understand, but she still warns, "If you wouldn't say it sober, don't say it when you're drunk. But if you have to say it, Never text it. Texting leaves a permanent record!"

4

PREGAME

Death by Google

• •

*He looks like the world's preppiest guy—polo shirt, Aber-
crombie jeans, short hair, just-shaved face. He's spent the
evening telling you about his scholarship to Stanford, his
dreams of helping refugee children in Africa, his two pet
cats. You're practically ready to go pick out wedding rings,
so when he asks if he can take you out some night, you
happily accept.*

That night, just out of idle curiosity, you plug his name

into Facebook. Bingo. Up pops his page—complete with pictures of himself, red-faced, completely trashed, swigging beer on a motorboat with a whole crew of frat brothers. Next picture: girl passed out on a sofa, with him and his friends standing around her, making obnoxious gestures. Next picture: him in a tux, standing next to a girl in a long white dress and a veil! Caption: "The happiest day of my life—my wedding day." Hello! Guess you won't be picking out those rings after all—but good thing you found out when you did.

Of course, what if you'd gone online and found out something you wish you hadn't? What if you found out that his mom's an alcoholic or his brother's in jail? These things might not stop you from dating him, but you'd probably feel awkward knowing things about him that he might not be ready to tell you. When you turn to the internet, are you being smart, or just nosy?

We've all Googled ourselves at some point. But should you do a search on a potential date? One thing is for sure— the information is out there. How you choose to use it is up to you.

HOW TO SLEUTH
LIKE A LAUREN

Lauren believes in being
prepared. In her opin-
ion, why should you limit
yourself? So, "before going out
with a guy, a girl should have as much
information as possible."

Face it—if it's on Google, it's public knowledge.
It's not like you're snooping through his underwear
drawer or something. As Lauren says, "If there's information out there, it's not wrong to look for it. And
if he has a MySpace or Facebook page, I'm all over that.
You can tell a lot about a person by the pictures they
choose and who their friends are."

"Of course, you never want to judge a person too
quickly, but you have to prescreen a little bit. I'm just
looking for warning signs and red flags. I don't want
to wait until halfway through the date to find out I'm
dating a crazy person. I don't want to wait until the
end of the night to find out he's married." Like our
Abercrombie guy. You'd be surprised how often that
happens.

He might even have done the same thing to you—

WHO SAID WHAT?

1. *Guys just need to know that they may have to wait a little bit, and they shouldn't be so desperate.*
2. *Every guy is a player until he finds the girl who makes him quit the game.*
3. *Dating is like a hobby.*
4. *Dating is awkward.*
5. *Dating is fun.*
6. *Dating is easy. Relationships are hard.*
7. *Dating is about quality, not quantity.*
8. *Looks aren't everything.*
9. *If bad traits show up early, that's a bad sign.*
10. *Flowers say, "I love you." Chocolates say, "I'm sorry."*
11. *Keep one guy on the back burner, another one on the front burner.*
12. *I could never have a one-night stand. I have too much respect for myself and my body.*
13. *You know what kinds of guys I like? Guys who are unavailable.*
14. *I've been boy crazy since I was a little kid.*
15. *Good boys are too easy. I want a bad boy.*
16. *We're not on different pages. We're in different libraries.*

ANSWER KEY: *1. W; 2. H; 3. L; 4. W; 5. L; 6. A; 7. W; 8. W; 9. W; 10. L; 11. H; 12. W; 13. L; 14. H; 15. A; 16. L*

Google is fair game. As long as you're not judging too harshly, there's not much harm in it, according to Lauren: "I like to think that I give every guy an equal chance when I meet him face-to-face." I just like to do my homework. Unless a guy is a wanted serial killer, what does he have to hide? And if I do find out something negative about a guy, I don't feel nosy. I feel smart."

HOW TO GET TO KNOW A GUY LIKE AUDRINA

Sometimes, looking a guy up on Google or Facebook can backfire. You can't actually know someone until you meet him face-to-face. At least, that's how Audrina feels when it comes to cyber-snooping. As she puts it, "I don't let a computer make up my mind."

"I believe the only way to get to know a person is to spend time with them," Audrina says. "You could look at their MySpace page or type their name into a search engine, but that only tells you part of the story. I don't want a computer to tell me how to think. That's why I never Google my dates. I want to make my own judgments on a guy."

If you're an Audrina, maybe you're more free-spirited. Doing research on your dates might feel a little weird. You might prefer just to go with the flow—if you meet a guy, go out with him, and he seems cool, then what do you care what kind of pictures are on his Facebook page? "I always feel like a snoop when I do [poke around online]," Audrina admits. "Maybe it's not as bad as going through his drawers or reading his e-mail, but I wouldn't want him to know I was doing it, so it definitely is sneaking. I'd just have trouble looking him in the eye when I knew I'd been digging around, trying to find his dirt."

Audrina hasn't always followed her own advice. She remembers the time she went out with a moto-cross racer named Kyle, and before their first date she innocently checked out his MySpace page: "It had all these pictures of him covered in tattoos, surrounded by tons of girls, and it talked about all the bones he had broken. From his profile, I expected him to be this crazy bad boy, but when I met him in person, he turned out to be the sweetest, nicest guy."

The reverse can happen too: "I've gone out with guys that everyone tells me are awesome, but when I sat down to talk to them, I realized they were sleazes. I don't need other people to tell me whether or not to like a guy, and I don't need a search engine to tell me if a guy can be trusted or not."

If you look hard enough at *anyone*, there's going to be a reason not to date them. Audrina would rather give her guys the benefit of the doubt. "I want to believe that the guys I meet are good people, and I trust them until they give me a reason not to. It's tempting to look people up, but I'm afraid that if I go looking for a reason not to trust people, I'll always find it. I'd rather give people the benefit of the doubt and come up with my own judgment."

What to Wear, When and How

• •

You've got the date. Now comes the hardest part—picking out what to wear! How many hours have you spent agonizing in front of the mirror, trying on outfit after outfit when getting ready to go out? Dress? Jeans? Tank top? Strapless? Sleeveless? Heels? Flats? Flip-flops? Boots? Earrings? Necklace? Ahhh! It's enough to make the sanest among us go crazy.

It gets even harder to decide what to wear when you

compare yourself to celebrities. How is it that they manage to look so amazing, even when they're wearing jeans and flip-flops? Well, we'll let you in on a little secret: if you had a clothing stylist, and a makeup artist, and a hairstylist, to help you get ready to go out at night, you'd look fabulous all the time too.

Until you either find fame or become rich enough to hire your own entourage, you're going to have to deal like the rest of us. But the girls of The Hills *can help take some of the stress out of the world's worst part of dating—getting dressed.*

HOW TO DRESS FOR A FIRST DATE LIKE A WHITNEY

Anyone who tells you that what you wear on a date isn't important is obviously living on another planet. We'd like to think that appearances don't matter, but let's be brutally honest—of course they do. So figuring out what to wear is not a decision Whitney takes lightly: "The clothes we wear are a means of expressing ourselves. The way that we wear clothes is part of what makes us all unique." The biggest mistake girls make is dressing in clothes that aren't really "them" when they go out. They might wear a sundress because they think it looks better than their favorite old jeans, but then they spend the entire night fidgeting with the dress, worrying about how it looks, and generally feeling uncomfortable. And believe me, all that stiffness *definitely* rubs off on your date, leaving him feeling uncomfortable too.

So, wear "you"! This doesn't mean you have to be boring, Whitney points out, "Your clothes say a lot about who you are, so you should always dress how you feel in the moment. If you're feeling a little shy and reserved, then maybe you should dress a little more conservatively. But if you feel like wearing something crazy and creative, then you should definitely go for it."

"Usually, you don't know the guy that well, and you have no idea where he's taking you," Whitney explains. "It's hard to know whether to dress for warm or cool, casual or dressy. The most important thing is to choose something you feel good in."

Whitney says the safest bet is always your favorite pair of jeans: "That way, you're covered even if he takes you someplace totally casual, but you can always dress jeans up quite a bit. Jeans and a swanky top or jacket are a good choice for almost any situation." Even if you're going to a fancy restaurant, you can still get away with dark-colored jeans paired with sandals or boots and a pretty top.

If you think the date is going to be slightly more upscale, then you might think about dressing it up a bit. "A casual cocktail-type dress is always appropriate with stockings, boots, heels, or flats. Again, it's whatever you feel good in." A simple cotton or wool dress without a lot of sparkles or embellishments is almost as versatile as jeans—wear it with ballet flats and a jean jacket and you're casual enough for dinner at a café or a walk on the beach. If you add heels and some jewelry, you can go to the theater or a swanky club.

"In the end, there's not one single way that all girls should dress," Whitney says. "The most important thing is that you like what you're wearing. If you're not feeling good about yourself, that feeling will come across to your date." And there's no bigger turnoff to a guy than a girl who isn't happy with herself.

HOW TO DRESS FOR A REPEAT DATE LIKE A HEIDI

Throughout this book, we've talked a lot about how to deal when you're first getting to know a guy. But what about after you've got him? Now he's your boyfriend and he's going to see you all the time. You might find yourself in a predicament like Heidi's: "Dressing for the first date is easy. The seventeen thousandth date is hard."

The nice thing about meeting someone new is that everything is fresh: all your funny stories, all your jokes, and all your clothes. You can safely grab your favorite black dress and ballet flats and know that he's never seen the outfit before. But as time goes on, the pressure to look good all the time builds. Heidi finds the challenge of looking good over a long period to be much more difficult than prepping for date number one: "You think it's hard dressing for someone you've only met once or twice? Try getting dressed for someone you're with every day. They've seen every single piece of clothing in your closet, twice!"

Of course you're going to relax some when you have a long-term boyfriend—you don't need to get out of your sweats just to watch TV with the guy you've been seeing for two years. But even a little effort makes a difference—think about hanging out with a guy who hasn't showered or shaved that day, ate onion pizza for lunch and didn't brush his teeth, and is sitting on your couch in his boxers and a holey T-shirt. You might still love the man, but you're probably not going to feel like snuggling up.

Even though she's been with Spencer for a long time, Heidi makes a special effort to look her best each and every time she goes out with him. "We've been on a million dates," Heidi says, "but I try to keep the 'Spirit of the First Date' alive. . . . One way that I keep things fresh for Spencer is by surprising him. If he's seen me in the same dress a few times, I'll go shopping by myself so that he's seeing me in something brand-new. And I always book a salon appointment, I always do my makeup, and I always have my nails done."

You don't have to look your very best *every* single time you see your guy. But at least shower, slap on the deodorant, and put on your *cute* sweats. Maybe go with the tank top instead of the giant old T-shirt of your brother's. Add a swipe of mascara and you're ready for a night of TV—almost no effort required.

As Heidi explains, "My relationship with Spencer is getting better and better, so why should I look worse and worse?"

The Justin Bobby Dictionary

The language of love has many dialects, but few are harder to interpret than that of the man affectionately known as Justin Bobby. Sensually blending poetic musings with poetic mumblings, Justin has constructed a vocabulary and a grammar all his own.

Audrina has spent several years trying to "speak Justin Bobby," with varying results. Subtle nuances can greatly affect meaning, making it difficult to know if he's feeling happy or sad, enraged or romantic. At times, it can be impossible to determine whether he's declaring undying love or breaking up with you.

After an exhaustive study, we've finally cracked the Justin Bobby code. Below are a few of his choice utterances, along with their English translations.

"The two of us can kick rocks and say peace."
Translates to:
"Perhaps it's time for us to bid fond adieu and pursue separate paths in life."

"Your friends don't fathom me at all, nor do I."
Translates to:
"Your acquaintances fail to take me seriously. I'm left with no alternative but to reciprocate."

"Games are for game boards, like Candy Land."
Translates to:
"My whole game is playing games while making it look like I'm not playing games."

"I get anxiety receptors in my ears, and I start going crazy."

Translates to:
"The voices are back."

"Truth and time tells all."
Translates to:
"The truth will come out in the distant future, so don't worry about the lies I tell tonight."

"Things should be happy and blissful and mellow."
Translates to:
"I'm afraid of commitment."

"I don't like having structure."
Translates to:
"I'm very afraid of commitment."

"If something's working, why ruin it by putting labels on it?"
Translates to:
"I am absolutely terrified of commitment."

"F your friends, literally."
Translates to:
"F your friends."

• • •

K.I.S.S. (Keep It Simple, Stupid)

* *

Hopefully, by this point in the dating guide, you're feeling better about dating, not worse. But you might be burying your head in the couch, trying to squash your racing thoughts: to text or not to text? Googling? Dressing? Drunk-dialing? Giving out your number? Who would have thought dating could be so complicated?

It's really not. Like anything else, the deeper you get into the subject, the more ideas come up. But if you're the type of girl who likes to keep it simple, Audrina and Whitney are in your corner. They've each boiled down their personal dating philosophies to one word.

It doesn't get any simpler than this.

HOW TO KEEP IT REAL LIKE A WHITNEY

Because she's a straightforward girl, Whitney's dating philosophy is "honesty."

"Honesty is really all there is," she says. "The only time I ever get in trouble is when I'm not being honest. The only time I feel embarrassed or uncomfortable is when I'm not honest. When I'm truthful, straightforward, and sharing my feelings, I never regret it."

"In the past, I haven't always allowed myself to open up," Whitney admits. "I kept my emotions to myself and didn't say what I meant. But if you're not honest about what you feel, you'll never get what you want. The only way to get what you need is to communicate."

Whitney is wary of people who put on an act when dating: "There's no act or game you can play that will lead you to a strong relationship. If a guy is looking for a girl that plays games, then that's not the guy I want to be with. You might get a guy's interest by being manipulative in the short term, but I'm not looking for the short term. I'm looking for something meaningful and lasting, and that starts with honesty. If a guy is turned off by real feelings, then that helps me weed him out right away." Say you and a new guy are trying to decide what movie to see. You're standing in front of the movie posters at the theater, looking over your options.

"Don't you hate cartoons?" the guy says, examining the poster for the newest Pixar flick. "They're always stupid."

"Um, yeah," you start to agree automatically, but

then you stop yourself. *Honesty*, you think. You take a deep breath. "Actually," you say slowly, "I love all those cartoons. *Shrek* was hilarious."

There—you've done it. You've been honest. Maybe he thinks you're a dork now, or that he's actually standing there with your younger sister or something, but at least you've been true to yourself. If he doesn't want to date you because you like cartoons, maybe *you* don't want to date him.

Whitney agrees: "I think most girls want what I want—a guy who tries to know you completely. To get that, you have to let it all out. Share your true feelings. You might scare away a few short-term guys, but that just means you'll waste less time with them. More importantly, you won't miss the rare long-term guy because you were too busy playing silly games."

HOW TO HAVE FUN
LIKE AN AUDRINA

Audrina's dating philosophy makes sense for an independent, free-spirited type like her: "fun."

"Don't take anything too seriously," she says. And,

Heidi's "How Not to Propose to a Girl"

- **Don't** propose until you have the parents' permission!

    "This makes them feel left out of the loop. It's the same as not asking them at all."

- **Don't** propose in a public place!

    "The girl may want to say no."

- **Don't** propose until you've had at least one discussion about weddings!

    "Does she want a huge wedding or private? Would she prefer a formal ceremony or an elopement in Vegas? These are things you should know *before* you pop the question."

- **Don't** propose unless you know the girl wants to get married!

    "The element of surprise is great, but some decisions need to be thought out!"

don't worry too much about each date, either. You're not marrying the guy that night! Just relax and have a good time meeting this new person. "You should never put too much pressure on one single date. Each date is really just a stepping-stone to figuring things out. You're learning how to date, you're learning about the type of person you want to spend your life with, and you're learning about yourself."

Weird as it may seem right now, the single years won't last forever. Eventually, you'll probably meet that Prince Charming and settle down. So why not enjoy dating while you can? Audrina says, "If you've dated a few people and learned from it, you'll be ready when you meet the one guy that you want to spend your life with. You'll know what it takes to keep a relationship going, because you'll have the experience."

"And if you keep an open mind and date a bunch of different types of people, you'll know it when the right guy comes along. If you've learned exactly what you want, you'll know it when you see it."

5

BOYFRIEND SHOPPING

Window-Shopping vs. Impulse Buys

. . . .

HOW TO SHOP FOR A BOYFRIEND:
A SHORT GUIDE

- **Do** *go with a classic style. Trends come and go, but nice, smart, and kind will last for years or even a lifetime.*

- **Don't** *grab the first one you see. Take your time, do* some comparison shopping. You can always go back later.

- **Do** look your purchase over carefully. Are there frayed edges? Uneven stitching? Is your purchase made of shoddy materials? Remember, you want quality over quantity.
- **Don't** overlook the smaller items other shoppers have shoved aside. Sometimes those are the best ones.
- **Do** keep your eyes peeled. You never know when a real bargain is going to pop up—even when you're not expecting it. Be ready to snare it before someone else does!

WHY WHITNEY BROWSES BEFORE SHE BUYS

Before you can find the perfect guy, Whitney says, "You have to do a lot of shopping around."

Whitney remembers a bit of relationship advice her mom gave her: "She told me you have to date a lot of people before you know what makes you happy. That's one of the great things about being young—you can shop around a little bit and find exactly what works."

It's not that Whitney is opposed to sticking with the same person, or the idea of love at first sight: "Of course, I think it's great when someone finds the right person, and they can stay committed to that one person for a long time. And it's definitely not impossible that you meet your soul mate when you're sixteen instead of twenty-six. But when you're young, it's difficult to know exactly who the right person is. I know that right now, I have no idea what kind of guy I'd marry." How can you know what you want if you haven't tried all the thirty-one flavors? If you always eat chocolate chip, you'll never know that maybe you like butter pecan even better.

"One of my friends has been going out with her boyfriend since sixth grade. She was *twelve* when she got together with him, and now they're twenty-three. She's spent almost half of her life with just one guy!"

"My friend always tells me that her relationship is going great, but I say, 'How do you know? You've never been with anyone else—what are you comparing it to?'"

"I'm not saying she'd be better off with someone else, but I think they'd both be better off to see a little more of the world and try some new things. They may be in an eleven-year committed relationship, but they have the dating experience of a couple of sixth-graders."

"Some would say that if you find a relationship that works at an early age, you don't waste any time with relationships that don't work. Others would say that it's the relationships that *don't* work that teach you the valuable skills and tools you need for the relationships that do."

You wouldn't buy an expensive pair of boots without trying them on first, and you wouldn't buy a new car without going for a test-drive. Before you get serious with a guy, look around, do some research, and

AUDRINA'S "ARE YOU A SERIAL DATER?" QUIZ

1. *Have you ever gone on two dates in one day?*

2. *Do you have a tough time remembering which outfit you wore on which date?*

3. *Have you ever run into a guy you were dating while you were out on a date with another guy you were dating?*

4. *Do you consider a week without a date "a dry spell"?*

5. *Have two different guys ever taken you to the same place for a date?*

6. *Do your friends struggle to keep all your dates straight?*

7. *Have you ever gone on a second date with a guy you knew you weren't interested in, just for something to do?*

8. *Have you ever accidentally called your date by another date's name?*

9. *Do you ever run into a guy and forget that you've actually gone out with him?*

10. *Have you ever had an entire phone conversation with a guy and not known exactly whom you were speaking with?*

If you answered yes to six or more of these questions, then you are officially a serial dater!

take your time. Impulse buys don't make good boy-friends.

What's in an Age?

* *

Whether you're out there robbing cradles or looking for a sugar daddy, it's hard to say that age doesn't matter. A lot of girls don't like to date younger guys, but what if a guy is smart, funny, and really, really cute? On the other hand, how old is too old? Old as your older brother? Old as your father? One year? Five years? Twenty years? Would you rather have a really mature younger guy or an older guy who isn't quite ready to grow up?

Here's our girls' take on the age debate.

HOW AUDRINA HANDLES THE AGE ISSUE

Wild child Audrina has dated both guys who were a little bit younger, and guys who were—well, *older.*

"I dated a model named Tyson, who was younger

than me, and I dated a drummer named Shannon, who was almost as old as my dad," Audrina admits. "That's an age range of about twenty years, so I guess the actual age isn't that important to me." Age is a lot more than just a number. Life experience can mature someone or keep him or her young.

"Shannon might have been a lot older, but touring with a band kept him young. He went to the same clubs, knew the same people, and listened to the same music as me," Audrina points out. "Through modeling, Tyson met a bunch of people and had a lot of experiences that someone his age usually wouldn't have. I had a lot of stuff in common with Shannon and Tyson, so it really didn't seem weird that we were different ages."

The only real age problem Audrina faced was with Tyson. It wasn't that he was younger . . . it was that he lied and said he was older: "Tyson told me he was four years older than he actually was. I care a lot more about the person than I do about what year they were born in, so there was no reason for him not to be honest. Lying is a much bigger turnoff than any age could ever be."

So maybe age does matter, but only a little bit. As Audrina says, "What matters is that you have a connection. What matters most is that you tell the truth!"

Dressing Up and Dressing Down: What to Wear in Any Situation

Beach Barbecue

- Stay away from the heavy makeup—you're going to be spending all day in the sun and water. Stick with fresh skin, a dab of tinted lip gloss, and water-proof mascara.
- Layer a simple cotton sundress over your bikini or wear the bikini top with a pair of cute board shorts.
- Leave the jewelry at home. Exceptions are simple hoop earrings, which look great with a tan and a bikini.
- Keep your hair loose, tie it up in a messy bun, or braid it in two braids, but avoid any hairstyle that's too sculptured or neat.

Meeting His Parents

- Keep the outfit conservative (duh!). No strapless, cleavage, or mini-anything. Think ballet flats, A-line dresses, small earrings, the pearls your grandma gave you. It's okay if you feel like Nancy Drew for one night.
- Keep the makeup conservative: go with rosy lip-stick instead of flame red, a swipe of brown or gray eye shadow instead of lime green.

Out at the Club

- You can never go wrong with sexy jeans, flats, boots, or heels, and a slinky top. Add some fun jewelry—this is the time to dig out the shoulder-length chandelier earrings.
- If you can, leave the heavy purse and jacket at home. You don't want to be carting those things around all night.
- If you're dying to break out the lime eye shadow, now is your chance. Glitter, orange lipstick—go for it.

Cooking Dinner at His Place

- Stick with your favorite comfy jeans, a cute tank top or T-shirt, and flip-flops.
- Keep the makeup simple: it gets hot in the kitchen and you're going to have a hard time being Betty Crocker with mascara rings under your eyes.
- Bring over an apron and wear it. Not only will you look adorable, you'll also protect your white T-shirt from spaghetti-sauce splatters.

WHY WHITNEY WON'T
GO YOUNGER

A lot of the time—not *all* the time—girls are ready to move on to the next step, in life or in a relationship, before guys are. So a guy five years older might be ready to settle down with one girl, while all the guys your age are still playing the field. You can sometimes get a more serious take on life by dating older guys, the way Whitney does.

"I just haven't met a younger guy who interests me," Whitney says. "It's a fact. Boys mature at a slower rate than girls. Girls grow into things a little faster, and they grow out of things a *lot* faster. In my experience, girls just tend to want different things than the guys their own age. I always find that I have an easier time relating to guys who are a few years older than me, while guys my own age seem to be stuck where I was several years ago." Remember those dances back in junior high where all the guys were about a foot shorter than the girls? This is the same thing, except that now the guys are taller. It's just that their brains haven't caught up.

Whitney also thinks that guys seem to have a different mind-set than girls at the same stage: "I just graduated from college, and most college guys were looking for the typical college relationship. Most recent college graduates aren't looking for anything much more serious, and in Hollywood it seems like *no* guy is looking for anything serious at all."

"That's fine, but I was always looking for something a little more sophisticated than that. I think I would have trouble going out with a twenty-two-year-old right now. Even though we'd be the same age, our heads would just be in two different places." Whitney might be interested in getting ahead in her career, finding an awesome apartment, and dating one guy. But all the boys her age might still be clubbing every night, partying every weekend, and dating a new girl every couple of days.

"I guess I would date a younger guy if he were mature far beyond his years," Whitney concludes, "but I haven't met that guy yet."

LAUREN'S YOUTHFUL OUTLOOK

As viewers of *The Hills* know, Lauren has dated someone younger than herself: Jason. In fact, when she was
seeing him, she never really even noticed the age difference.

"Jason was a good example of a guy who never
really seemed young," Lauren says. "He acted as old as
most of my friends, he seemed at least as old as me,
and he looked way older. I probably wouldn't have
thought that I would have been interested in a younger
guy before I started seeing Jason, but once we got into
it, I never really thought about it." Lauren was more
focused on the person than on the numbers.

"So I guess it's really not about age, it's
about life experience. There are college
guys who are twenty-two who are
still going to fraternity
parties every night
and basically acting
like boys. Then there
are guys who are nine-
teen, have jobs, and have
their whole lives together.
Their actual age doesn't mat-

ter, because they're just in completely different places in their lives." People who have moved around and seen a lot of the world sometimes seem older than those guys who've spent their whole life hanging out with the same group of friends, in the same town they grew up in.

But still, if Lauren had to choose, "for the most part, I tend to like guys who are a few years older, but if it's the right guy, age doesn't really matter."

HOW HEIDI HANDLES AGE

Older guys are one thing. Guys old enough to remember the Summer of Love are an- other. It can be hard to date someone who is in a totally different stage of his life. As much as you want maturity and so- phistication, you don't want to be stuck with someone who wants to get married and buy a house while you're still figuring out what to declare as a major. Heidi, an experienced guy evaluator, agrees: "I date older guys, but not too old."

According to Heidi, there's nothing wrong with a few extra years of experience—but maybe not extra *decades*. "I think women should be with older guys, but not so old that they could be their fathers. It seems every guy wants to date a young girl, but when the difference is too big, you have to wonder what is wrong with the guy. Someone who is twelve, fifteen, or twenty years older is obviously going to have a different set of experiences. Why would they want to go out with someone who hasn't shared any of those? Why can't they relate to someone their own age?"

The romantics among us might insist that when a couple is in love, age is irrelevant, but Heidi takes a slightly more cynical point of view: "When I see a much older guy with a much younger girl, I just assume that the guy's heart isn't truly into it. The poor girl might be madly in love with him, but the guy is probably just with the girl for a little bit of arm candy. When the two of you grew up in different times, with different movies and music, and basically different worlds, what could you possibly have to talk about?" Of course, love across the years is possible—anything is possible. But we can't deny it's going to be harder. If your true love is the same age as Steven Tyler, then you and he are going to have to really work to relate to each other. A large helping of understanding will be invaluable.

Heidi has taken her own advice and chosen a guy who is older, but not ancient. Beautiful blond boy Spencer is just the right age, according to her. "Spencer is about three years older, and that seems perfect. We have all the same references and like all the same things, which is good," Heidi says. "But Spencer also has a three-year head start on me in terms of figuring out his life and what he wants, which is great. I value having the opinion of someone with just a little more wisdom and experience—I'm just glad I don't have to date a really old guy to get it!"

Best Hookup Music

Lauren
Death Cab for Cutie
Jimmy Eat World
Oasis
Foo Fighters, "Everlong"

Whitney
Al Green, "Let's Stay Together"

Audrina
Marvin Gaye, "Let's Get It On"

Anything by Phil Collins
Scorpions, "Winds of Change," and Smashing
    Pumpkins, "Tarantula," when with Justin

Heidi
Anything by Norah Jones
Anything by Barry White
Etta James, "At Last"
And, for special occasions, Heidi Montag

● ● ●

LC ON BJ: BJ OR BJJ?

For the past couple of years, Lauren has had an on-again, off-again relationship with Brody Jenner. It works like this: every time you think it's off, it's on again, and every time you think it's on, it's off again.

Guessing the status of Lauren and Brody has been a great source of entertainment for all their friends. Barbecue on Thursday: Lauren says hi to Brody, but then huddles in the corner with Audrina for the rest of the party. Brody might as well be a sofa for all the notice she's taking. Birthday house party on Sunday: You can barely see the air between Lauren and Brody all night as they stick to each other like glue.

But even harder than nailing down their status was

getting either of them to give you a straight answer. Luckily, the suspense is over. Lauren finally explains how she really feels about Brody, and what he really is to her: BF or BFF?

LAUREN'S BRODY LOWDOWN

"Brody and I are just friends," Lauren maintains, then admits, "friends who make out sometimes." Okay, Lauren, so that would be friends with benefits, right?

Lauren doesn't know what it is about her relationship with Brody, but everyone around her has always been obsessed with putting a label on it: "The whole time we were dating, people were telling me to be careful. When we were just friends, people were telling us we should date. I think other people spend a lot more time thinking about our relationship than either of us does."

Lauren and Brody really only dated for a short time, but that doesn't stop nearly everyone else from offering opinions: "People I barely know come up to me and give me advice on Brody. I'm like, 'Thanks, but who are you?'" It can be hard to have a relationship while being filmed on reality TV—how would you like all your romantic angst broadcast to a billion eager eyes every week?

Despite the media pressure, Lauren and Brody have been close for a long time—partly because they just genuinely have a lot in common: "I know that we do have good chemistry. I think that's because we're alike in a lot of ways. But I also know that when we dated, we did almost nothing but fight and argue all the time. I think that's because we're alike in a lot of ways too."

"We did date for a little while, but we were never boyfriend and girlfriend. We staggered on in that in-between state and never quite made it to the next level." The Heidi-Spencer-Lauren drama didn't exactly help her relationship with Brody: "A lot of what we fought about had to do with Heidi and Spencer. So now that they're out of both of our lives, it seems like we might not have any problems, but I don't think that's true. There's always going to be things you disagree on, and if two people can't work things out without arguing, then it probably means they're not a good match."

Lauren and Brody have no regrets. "We really did give dating a try," says Lauren, "and it just didn't work. But I love having Brody as a friend, and we know that *does* work. We're both perfectly happy as friends and nothing more, no matter how it looks to other people. I admit that I sometimes light up a little when Brody's around, and he does make me laugh, but then again, so does Lo."

Even though you once hooked up or he happens to be a guy doesn't mean you have to either date him or drop him. Strange as it may seem, guys and girls can actually be real platonic friends—even *after* they've broken up. It takes a little work to get past whatever hurt feelings or sexual tension might be left over, but you wouldn't want to drop a really awesome friend just because you once made out in your parents' den.

Lauren and Brody have actually been boyfriend-girlfriend, but a more awkward situation is that "accidental" hookup with a really good guy friend. Let's say that you and your buddy Michael have been best friends forever. You guys played naked in the kiddie pool when you were in nursery school (those days are over, thank God), held bug-eating contests in second grade, and spent hours watching *Brady Bunch* reruns when you were both sick with the chicken pox in middle school. Now you're older, and even though you try not to, you can't help noticing that all of a sudden, Michael isn't just Michael—he's also a *guy*, and a really hot one too. Recently, you've gotten the idea that he might be thinking the same thing about you. The tension builds and builds until one day you find yourselves making out in your kitchen where you both were looking for a snack after school. Now things are weird between you. You avoid each other, and when you do accidentally meet, you don't know what to say, where to look, or what to do with your hands. And it's obvious he feels the same way, if not more so.

What should you do? You don't want to lose this relationship, but maybe the hookup just wasn't right for either of you. But you know that you *were* right as friends. So you need to try to get back to the "friends" place you were before. The next time you see him, you should ask to talk with him alone. Then just be straight: Tell him that you've felt totally weird since that day in the kitchen and you don't like feeling awkward around him. Then ask him if he feels the same way.

Lauren and Brody have managed to hang on to their friendship, in spite of (or because of) their many hookups. But, "in the end, Brody is just another friend, like Whitney, Lo, or Audrina," Lauren says. There is one notable exception: "The only difference is, I haven't made out with them."

The Stephen Saga

* *

You know that one guy you've known forever? You guys grew up together and you totally understand each other. He's like your brother—except that he's definitely not. Being around him is like putting on your favorite old slippers— relaxing, totally comfy, and utterly familiar.

For Lauren, the old-slippers guy has always been Stephen Coletti.

Lauren and Stephen have remained good friends over the years, and on occasion they've even been, well, more than friends. But every time they looked destined to be together, something (or, just as often, someone) pushed them apart. And yet, every time they decided to give up on romance and just be friends, something would happen to reignite that spark.

Here's what Lauren has to say about her lifelong relationship with Stephen, why she'll always love him, the ups and downs of their past, and the possibility of their future.

HOW LAUREN KEPT A CRUSH ALIVE

"With Stephen," Lauren explains, "it's a comfortable love. We grew up together, and we were childhood friends, so we'll always be close. He knows me as well as anyone, and I can be completely myself around him. But, over the years, we've occasionally taken our relationship to a place of more than friends." With a guy as tall, dark, and handsome as Stephen, who could blame her?

Depending on whom you ask, the "more than friends" history either started back when Lauren was in seventh grade, when she dated Stephen for one week, or when she was eighteen. "For whatever reason, it never really worked out, and not all of that had to do with Kristin Cavallari. Whether we were both seeing someone else or both single, it seemed like it was just never meant to progress past the 'friends' stage."

But just when Lauren thinks she's okay with that, something happens to kick the sexual tension up a notch again. "I have definitely fallen in and out of love with Stephen over the years. I start to like him again, and I think that maybe he likes me. I convince myself that things are going to be different this time. Then, just when I get my hopes up, I realize that it's the same thing. We're just falling into the same crush routine, and it always ends the same way."

So what is it about Stephen that Lauren finds so irresistible? "Stephen's real magic is that he's a nice guy, without being a Nice Guy. He's genuinely a very good person, he's a good listener, and he's truly sweet. But Stephen's different than your average Nice Guy, because he's not overly nice. He's not a doormat, he's not annoyingly attentive, and he's not boring. That's his whole secret: every girl wants to date a nice guy, but nobody wants to date a Nice Guy."

To this day, Lauren is asked by family, friends, and complete strangers if she might ever end up with Stephen, or if she thinks she'll ever get over him. "Part of me will always love Stephen. I'll never have that sort of history with anyone else, and when I'm around him, he makes me feel like I'm still in high school." Lauren lets herself enjoy that thought for a moment, before crashing back to earth: "But I'm not in high school anymore."

Lo's Philosophy

• •

Doesn't it seem unfair that when guys date all sorts of girls, they're called players, but when girls do the same thing, they're called . . . well, something not as nice. What kind of double standard is that?

The truth is, although a lot of girls (and guys!) date to find that one special person, not everyone wants to settle down. Some girls just like going out, meeting guys, maybe hooking up, maybe not. All they want is to have a little fun. Snaring the Boyfriend is just not important to them. In fact, some girls—such as Lauren's longtime Laguna Beach friend, Lo—actually do not want a boyfriend. If a guy starts getting too serious (example: "So, when do I get to meet your parents? How about Thanksgiving?"), Lo actually takes that as a sign to run far away as fast as she can.

Lo has never been afraid to speak her mind or share her unique opinions. Here's her particular take on the value (or burden) of having a serious boyfriend.

HOW TO DODGE A BOYFRIEND LIKE A LO

If this book were about Lo's relationship advice, it wouldn't be a book. Lo has only one word for girls who are on the hunt for a boyfriend: "Don't."

Lo does not spend a lot of time wondering how she's going to meet guys or start a new relationship: "I just really don't like having boyfriends. I'm never looking for something long-term. I get bored way too easily." In Lo's world, there's no sense in trying yourself down to one guy when so many other yummy ones are out there to meet.

It's not that Lo doesn't have any guy friends—or guy friends with benefits. "I always have a few guys I hang out with, but hanging out is very different than going out," she explains. "It's more casual than a relationship or dating, and I don't go out of my way to make things too serious. Hanging out with someone is a lot less pressure, and it's more fun."

When the guy starts circling too close—getting pouty if she won't see him two nights in a row, keeping tabs on whom else she sees when she goes out, hinting that he'd like to go exclusive—Lo starts to lose interest: "A serious relationship is not what I'm looking for right now, so I end up pulling away. I start ignoring texts and stop returning phone calls until the guy gets the point."

Living in Hollywood isn't exactly conducive to the good old find-a-nice-guy, settle-down, buy-a-house-with-a-white-picket-fence, get-a-dog, have-two-kids routine, Lo says: "Some of it is probably the city we're in. Most of the guys you meet out at bars and clubs aren't looking for anything too long-term, they're just looking to hook up. But I can't complain too much about Hollywood boys because we keep going back to them! They may be players, but it hasn't stopped us from going out and meeting them."

"I think it really just comes down to the stage we're at in our lives. We're young, and this is the time to have fun and not turn everything into a huge commitment. I just try to have a good time, take each day as it is, and not take anything too seriously." An added benefit to not taking things too seriously is that Lo gets to avoid all the annoying drama that comes with high-pressure, serious relationships. While other girls are off slamming doors and yelling at their boyfriends on the phone and then holding tearful reconciliations later, Lo can focus on having a good time.

But just because she's not in boyfriend mode right now doesn't mean that she rules out any chance of a long-term relationship down the line. "I have confidence that when the time is right and the guy is right, I'll know it. I don't think it will be hard to transition to something more serious. But right now, all my relationships are casual and fun, and that's fine with me."

Can Your Best Friend Be Your Boyfriend?

* *

Having a guy as your best friend can be awesome. He loves the same movies and music as you, and he always manages to call just when you need to be cheered up. You can tell him all your dating angst, and he can give the male perspective. In return, you advise him on all the mysterious ways of women and pat his back when he gets dumped by that girl he was crushing on. So why not combine the best of both worlds? How much easier would your life be if your best guy friend were also your boyfriend?

Sounds good, right? Well, before you take a running

leap into that pool, just stand back for one second. You've probably seen enough Hollywood romantic comedies to know what happens when platonic friends try to become something more. My Best Friend's Wedding, *anyone? If the romance wasn't there to begin with, can you spark it now? If things don't work out, are you willing to risk losing your boyfriend and your best friend on the same day?*

Here's what our girls think about taking things beyond "just friends."

WHY WHITNEY WOULD NEVER DATE HER BEST FRIEND

Leave it to Whitney to offer a little clear-eyed, hard-headed perspective on the subject. "Best friends and boyfriends are two different things," Whitney says. Doesn't get any simpler than that.

Whitney's best male friend is Josh. Whitney has strong feelings for him, but strong feelings aren't always enough: "He's sweet, smart, and I love him—but not like that. There's a reason why we've never gotten together. He's just not my type, and I really don't think I'm his. If there were an ounce of attraction, we would know by now. It's just not there, and I don't think that it ever will be."

Of course, it's tempting to try to turn that boy friend into a boyfriend. I mean, you have the same interests, values, and beliefs, so why waste all that perfection? Well, if love were a math equation, it would work every time. But love is more like an art project—big and messy, with a distinct lack of straight lines and right angles. You can't be with someone "like that" if you don't have that impossible-to-define, intangible *something*—that spark when you see him that makes you want to wrestle him to the ground right then and there.

Whitney explains, "I've heard stories from a couple of people who've turned friendship into romance, and it is a nice idea. I just know that I can tell if a guy sparks romantic feelings for me pretty early on. If I'm going to have feelings for a guy, it's not going to take years for me to realize it."

"I hate to say it," Whitney says, "but I don't know if men and women can truly be friends when they're attracted to each other. True friends are happy only being friends. When one person wants something more from the other or is secretly trying to push the relationship into a different direction, than that's not true friendship. If a guy I thought was my friend was actually spending time with me hoping for a physical relationship, I'd be mad, not flattered. For me, romance and friendship are just two separate things, and I like to keep them separate."

HEIDI'S FRIENDSHIP PHILOSOPHY

Even though she's skeptical, Whitney is at least willing to consider the idea of hooking up with your guy friend. But Heidi takes a firmer stance: girlfriend, it just can't happen: "Men and women can't go from being friends to dating because men and women can't really be friends in the first place."

This sounds harsh, but Heidi isn't being jaded. She explains, "I don't think that two people can be friends without the attraction getting in the way. So either it's not true friendship, and one person is always trying to make it into something more, or there's absolutely zero attraction, and zero chance of romance."

"The best scenario is that you go out with the person you're attracted to, and *then* they become your best friend. It's hard to find, but that's what Spencer and I have. I can tell him anything, and he knows what I'm thinking before I think it. He never judges me and he always understands me."

So while Heidi stomped on the idea of having a relationship with your guy friend, she offers a better alternative: "I don't really think that your best friend can become your boyfriend. But in the best relationships, your boyfriend will become your best friend."

Exclude Your Friend's Ex, No Exceptions

There are several big no-no's in the dating world: Never bring up your old loves on the first date. Never order the French-onion soup. Never call him "honey babe" in front of his buddies. Never let your friends date jerks. Never suggest he forgo poker night to watch Sex and the City *reruns with you. And never date a friend's ex!*

Yeah, yeah, it can be hard. Maybe you've been crush-

ing on him for years. And now they're finally broken up—
all's fair in love and war, right? Wrong. Unless you don't
want to have any more friends.

Exes are a delicate topic. Here's how to navigate that
minefield.

WHOM WHITNEY WON'T DATE

On the subject of dating
exes, Whitney has her
mind made up: "I don't
want my friends dating
my ex, so I won't date my
friend's ex." Remember the Golden
Rule you learned back in first grade? Then
it meant don't kick people on the playground if you
don't want to be kicked. We're a few years beyond that,
but the principle remains the same.

Whitney feels strongly on the subject: "If my
friend called me and asked if she could go out with one
of my exes, ninety-nine out of a hundred times I would
say no, and the hundredth time I'd be lying. The only

reason I'd say yes was if I was too embarrassed to admit that I still had feelings for the guy. I just know it would hurt too much. So whether I say no, or say yes and mean no, know that I really mean no." If you mean no, then say no. If you say yes, you'd better mean it. It's hard to expect your friends to be mind readers, even your best buds.

Breaking up is hard enough. A lot of times the only comfort you have is knowing that your friends are there for you no matter what. When the people you thought you could count on are actually sneaking around with your ex-boyfriend, it makes a bad situation into crying-on-your-bed bad.

"It works the other way too," Whitney explains. "After I broke up with David, one of his friends called me a few times and asked to get together with me. I don't know if he was just being nice, or if he was asking me on a date, but either way, it just didn't feel right. David and I were still working things out, and there were still a lot of emotions there. I knew David wouldn't be happy to hear I was out being social with one of his buddies. I knew he *really* wouldn't be happy to hear I was out being romantic with one of his buddies, and I had no desire to hurt David." Whitney is a woman of her word. She simply thanked his friend for calling, then politely turned down his invitation.

Whitney concludes, "No matter what the circumstances, and no matter what your friend says, show her respect and leave the ex alone. Don't make her relive the pain of the breakup. Don't embarrass her by making her admit she still has feelings for her ex. Remember, she just lost a boyfriend. Don't make her lose a best friend too."

WHY HEIDI WOULD NEVER DATE A FRIEND'S EX

Sure, Heidi says, go right ahead and date your friend's ex—if you don't want her as a friend anymore. "The only time it's ever okay to go out with your friend's ex," Heidi says, "is if you want to end that friendship."

Heidi believes that no matter how good a friend you think you are to someone, *no* friendship can sustain dating the ex: "You have to be realistic going in. If you think you can't live without the guy, ask yourself if you can live without the friend. You're basically making a trade. It's hard to find a boyfriend that you really like, but it's harder to find a friend you can totally trust. Are you really willing to make that trade-off?"

Of course, if the breakup was all you—like *really* all you, right from the beginning—then handing an ex off to a friend can be much easier. You weren't crazy about the guy, so maybe she'll like him better. But that's really the only situation were ex-dating can work. If he had anything at all to do with the breakup, it's really going to hurt when you spot him and your (former) friend holding hands while gazing dreamily at each other over triple-venti caramel lattes.

Unfortunately, a lot of girls are perfectly willing to take a chance on dating a friend's ex, and a lot of girls have lost their boyfriend *and* their best friend in close succession. Heidi says that girls who act surprised by this are only acting: "Girls are aggressive and girls are smart. Most girls know exactly what they're doing when they go for someone's ex. So before you think about dating someone's ex, you better be sure you're ready to face the consequences."

AUDRINA'S EX POLICY

Audrina says, "I would totally date my friend's ex . . . after ten years." That's about the amount of time it would take for all those old hurt feelings and lingering romantic memories to finally die.

"Dealing with exes is just so weird," Audrina explains. "I have friends that have feelings for old boyfriends even after they've been broken up for two or three years. They'll hear a song or see an old movie, and all of a sudden they're thinking about their ex. I understand that, which is why I always stay away from my friends' ex-boyfriends." People break up for all kinds of reasons. Maybe your friend and her ex broke up because she was going to college. Obviously, they're probably still going to have some feelings for each other. Or maybe he cheated on her. She's going to have even stronger feelings about you going out with him after that.

By the way, the same thing goes for your ex's own friends, Audrina reminds us. "Justin's friend Derek had a little crush on me. Justin would act like he didn't care, but I know he cared so much. When Justin found out that Derek was interested in me, he asked how I would feel if he started talking to Lauren. He was right—I would hate to think about one of my friends being with him. That's why I'll never go out with one of his friends."

"I'm not saying I'll *never* go out with my ex's friend or my friend's ex," Audrina says. "It will just take ten years before that's okay."

So according to Audrina, it *is* okay to date your friend's ex-boyfriend. If the breakup happens tomorrow, we can plan your first date for somewhere around 2019.

WHY LAUREN LEAVES EXES ALONE

One more thing. In addition to not dating your friend's ex, or your ex's friends, you also shouldn't date your ex yourself. This little nugget comes straight from the expert herself: Lauren Conrad. "No one should ever date your ex," she says, "especially not you."

Lauren has a simple rule when it comes to past boyfriends: "Once an ex, always an ex. You go out with a guy, give it everything you have, and try to make it work. If it doesn't work, you're done. Let it go and get on with your life. In a few days, weeks, months, or years, you'll miss your ex. You'll remember all the good things about him and none of the bad. But remember, there was a reason why you went through that painful breakup. There was a reason why you finally told yourself you couldn't take it one more day. The truth is, all those reasons are still alive in your ex. As much as we wish we could, you can't really change guys." There's always a chance that your ex might show up in your life again, swearing that he's changed his ways, he's totally different now, just give him another chance. And you might be tempted. But if you follow Lauren's advice, you won't go down that road.

According to Lauren, your ex-boyfriend can never be your boyfriend again, but he can be your friend: "All that work you put into the relationship and all that time you spent getting to know each other didn't go to waste. You can still share each other's problems, you can still share each other's jokes, and you can even talk about your current relationship if you feel comfortable. You just can never get back that romance."

6

THE DATE

Safety in Numbers

Did you ever think what a huge advantage guys usually have on a first date? Most of the time, they make the plans, pick you up, decide where you're going to eat, what you're going to do afterward. And let's be honest—a lot of the time, if there's going to be any romantic action, we're waiting for them to make the first move.

Come on, ladies! It's 2008, not 1954. So why are we still letting the guys make all the decisions? You decide what happens in your work life, your school life, and your home life, right? Why not in your dating life?

Here are some tips for feeling more comfortable on a first date, and putting some of the control back in your corner.

HOW AUDRINA MAKES DATING A TEAM SPORT

After long experience, Audrina has developed a solid first-date rule: "I always make the first date a group date."

"When a new guy asks me out, I try to avoid the solo date," she explains. "It's just a lot of pressure and it can be awkward. There's nothing worse than sitting down in a restaurant and figuring out that you have absolutely nothing to say to a guy before you've even ordered appetizers." Then the awkward silence sets in. He fiddles with his fork. You take a sip of water. You both look around the restaurant. Then you sneak a look at him—just as he's sneaking a look at you. Oops. You both look away, fast. The silence stretches out . . . and out . . . and out. Everyone at the tables around you

is laughing and talking and shoveling in food, obviously having a much better time than you are. Then he says, "It's so hot today." The old weather comment—a sure sign things are *not* going well.

Audrina would rather just avoid this entire situation. Having friends around is relaxing and takes a lot of the pressure off: "I try to have him come meet me out somewhere. This is great because I'm with my friends, so I don't have to worry about if he's a nice guy or not. And if he's boring, I can just talk to my friends and disappear into the group. First dates can be hard work, but I know my friends are a good time. If you can't laugh and have a good time with *my* friends, that's a bad sign."

It's kind of like meeting the parents, just not as
high pressure. You wouldn't want to date someone who
doesn't seem to fit in with your life, right? So, let's say
he does wind up coming out. Everyone has a good time,
your friends like him. Then comes the next test—his
friends. Whom a guy chooses to hang out with says a
lot about him. If you think they're all jerks, chances
are your new boy is a jerk too. "When guys come to
meet you and your friends, they always bring their
friends," Audrina explains. "You can get to know a guy
really fast when you meet his friends. You can see if he
has a strong group who really care about him, or if he
just has fake 'going out' friends. And I always listen to
the stories they tell about him. At the start of the night,
a guy's friends only tell stories to make him look good,
but by the end of the night, the truth comes out. Sometimes, a guy's buddies will tell you things the first night
that the guy wouldn't tell you in a hundred years." Forget all the sweet stories—the dirt is the stuff you want
to listen to.

Dating Do-Over

What if that first date didn't go so well? The guy had potential, but the whole evening just wasn't fun. First it was

raining, and you didn't like the outfit you'd chosen, which made you a little cranky. Then the first thing he announced when he picked you up was that he was totally tired. You were annoyed that he ordered your food for you while you were in the bathroom, and he told the waiter to bring the check when you still wanted dessert.

So, should you drop him? Chalk up another wasted night and move along? Well, not according to Whitney. She thinks that people feel too much pressure to make the first date the perfect date. Here's her strategy to get to know someone in twice the time, and with half the stress.

Lauren and Audrina's Double-Bad Double-Date Timeline

6:15   Lauren and Audrina get ready for a blind double date. They wonder what the guys will be like. Lauren thinks it will go poorly, which she interprets to mean it will go well. "When you're expecting it to be bad, it turns out good," Lauren explains.

6:20   Just in case it's *not* love at first sight, they try to choose a code word, but have trouble coming up with anything subtle. Audrina has a small zit on her forehead, and talking about it will be their secret signal that the date is going badly. It's a nice idea, but when girls discuss their acne, guys can usually figure out that the date's not going well.

7:00   Lauren has made it clear that she doesn't like it when guys bring her flowers. Sure enough, her date, Zach, arrives bearing a bouquet. That's strike one, but he gets points for trying.

7:30   Dinner comes, and Joey, Audrina's date, discusses his diet. He never eats carbs and avoids fat, but tonight he's decided to cheat a little.

Audrina's into tattoos, leather, and motorcycles, so it's lucky that she's matched with the wild one.

8:15   Joey busts out the signature bad-date line: "What's your sign?"

Silence ensues.

8:16   Joey changes the subject from astrology to another of his interests: grocery shopping. The silence is deafening.

9:00 Lauren defies her carb-counting company by ordering dessert. Joey ventures one bite and blurts out, "That's heaven in my mouth."
That's strike two.

10:45 The boys follow Lauren and Audrina to Area, where the conversation continues to drag. After a few big yawns, Lauren explains, "I'm not bored, I'm just exhausted."
Boredom was two hours ago.

11:00 The drinks bill comes, and it's not small. One of the boys sprints for the bathroom, and the other just turns around and pretends not to notice. The waitress stands there tapping her foot, until Audrina mercifully puts down her credit card for the entire tab.
And that's strike three.

11:05 The date is officially going badly, so Audrina breaks out the secret code: "Lauren, my zit's getting bigger."
Drastic times call for drastic measures.

11:06 After Audrina's Code Red, the girls hurry out of the club and hail a taxi. Before the

guys can get any ideas about number ex-
changes, repeat dates, or good-night kisses,
the girls dive into the taxi and speed away.

Sometimes, when you're expecting it to
be bad, it's good. Other times, expecting
bad leads to simply bad.

● ● ●

HOW TO TAKE YOUR TIME
LIKE A WHITNEY

Whitney thinks everyone deserves a second chance—
even dweeby guys who make up nicknames for you on
the first date.

It helps that Whitney has pretty good intuition
when it comes to guys: "Under normal circumstances,
I can tell if a guy is trustworthy, nice, and nice to be
around. But a first date isn't a normal circumstance—
it's a nerve-racking, high-pressure situation where
everyone is trying too hard. That's not an easy place to
make a good first impression, so you have to give a guy
a second chance."

"I recently went out on a date and there was zero

chemistry," Whitney recalls. "He was nice and attractive enough, but we just never clicked. We only had date conversation, we never had *real* conversation. I thought I was never going to see him again, but then he called and asked me out again. I can't say why, but I agreed to give him one more try. I was expecting to go out with the same guy, with the same awkward conversation, but then a surprising thing happened. When he picked me up, he was a whole new person." Sometimes, you just have to get through the awkwardness to find the real person underneath. I mean, let's be honest—it's not all on the guy's side. How many times have you spent an entire evening spouting inane comments that mean nothing, just because you were tense and nervous?

Whitney's guy deserved his second chance. With the pressure of the first date over, he was more relaxed, more secure, and a lot more fun. As Whitney puts it, "He was *himself*. He wasn't so concerned about always saying the right thing, so he wasn't talking out of his butt. Just knowing that I liked him enough to see him again made all the difference." All this guy needed, apparently, was a little boost of confidence. That helped him relax enough to have fun.

"So when I say yes to a date, I'm really saying yes to *two* dates—presuming he likes *me* enough to ask me out again! This is good because it forces me to be a little choosier about who I go out with. Rather than asking, 'Is this someone I would want to sit through dinner and a movie with?' the question becomes 'Is this someone I would want to sit through *two* dinners and *two* movies with?' That helps screen out a lot of people."

"It also takes the pressure off the guy. It gives your date a chance to settle in and be himself. He doesn't have the pressure of being thrilling and charming and hilarious in the span of a few hours. He gets two chances to show me his best side. He gets a do-over."

"Finally, it takes the pressure off of me. I know that this date is just a run-through. The second date is the one that really counts." After two dates, if the chemistry still isn't sparking, well, maybe it's time to cut him loose.

Whitney advises to "show a little patience when you go out with a guy. Anyone can have an off night, so give a guy a second chance. But if he doesn't bring his A-game on the second date, then sorry! A girl's patience only goes so far. That's why I always give a guy a second chance . . . but never a third!"

Lauren's Bad-Date Timeline

9:15   Lauren, Audrina, Jarett, and Derek are enjoying drinks at Lola's. Things seem to be going great, until Derek suddenly declares girls from Los Angeles "trashy."

Lauren points out that she's a girl and she's from Los Angeles. He can't quite figure out why this would be offensive.

9:30   Derek mentions that he used to be a janitor, which Lauren finds sort of charming. Then he describes in detail what he used to clean toilets, which Lauren finds considerably less charming.

Lauren and Audrina are praying he doesn't want to go out after drinks.

9:31   He wants to go out after drinks. They decide on Les Deux. Derek begins chanting, "Let's Les Deux it! Let's Les Deux it!"
Lauren is thinking, "Let's Les Don't."

10:10   At Les Deux, Derek refers to women as "broads." When Lauren tries to explain that girls don't love being called broads, he explains that he's been "calling chicks 'broads'" his entire life.
Derek and Lauren just can't seem to agree on anything.

11:00   Derek corners Lauren and tells her that he "can't stop thinking about" her, and that he likes her "more than anyone" he's ever met. "Is that psychotic?" Derek wonders.
Finally, something Lauren and Derek can agree on!

● ● ●

Heidi's Secret Language

· ·

You call your friends before the date when you're getting dressed. You call them after the date to give them the details on how it went. So why isn't there a way to get your friends' advice during the date, when it could actually help you?

Dating expert Heidi has been through some really bad dates—and sometimes, she needed her girlfriends there with her. So she came up with a secret code that lets you keep your friends with you at all times. Whether you're at dinner, at the movies, or alone with your date, you can always keep your best advisers close at hand.

You'll never have to brave another date alone!

HOW HEIDI CRACKS THE DATING CODE

"Girls need their girlfriends," Heidi says, "one hundred percent of the time."

Heidi remembers missing her girlfriends during the first stages of a relationship: "When I used to date new guys, I'd always want to get my friends' opinion of

him right away. And when my friends go out with a new boy, I don't want to wait to hear how it went, I want to know how it's going!"

Heidi got the idea for a code when Audrina was going out with a guy named Danny. Audrina wasn't sure exactly how she felt about him, so she didn't want to wait until the next morning to get Heidi's feelings and opinions. "I knew Audrina was going to dinner," Heidi says, "so I came up with a code where I would ask her to tell me about the food, but really, Audrina would be talking about her date. That way, I could call her in the middle of the date, and she could tell me every-thing without telling him anything."

Here's how it works:

The food is bad = This guy is terrible. Get me out of here ASAP.

The food is bland = This guy is so boring, I want to cry.

The food is greasy = This guy is slimy, and his hair needs an oil change.

The food is good = I'm having a good time. Already thinking about date two.

The food is amazing = I'm having a great time. Already picking out baby names.

We're having dessert = Don't wait up for me. This could take a while.

To Kiss or Not to Kiss?

* *

Right from the start, you could tell this one was going to be awesome. He picked you up right on time, bearing a giant bouquet of wildflowers. He took you to an out-of-the-way place by the beach where the two of you ate clams and lobster, taking turns feeding each other in your best romantic-comedy style. Afterward, you walked on the beach and you found yourself telling him all about your family, your friends, and your plans for the future. Now you're sitting in his car, in front of your house, and that big date moment—the one you both have been thinking about basically all night—has finally come. The kiss. Should you do it? If you like this guy, maybe you should. If you really *like this guy, maybe you shouldn't.*

Here's what the girls have to say about kissing on the first date—and how they think it affects the chances of a second date.

HOW TO HANDLE THE KISS QUESTION LIKE A HEIDI

For a party girl, Heidi has strict standards: "Kissing on the first date isn't a question. I never even kiss on the *second* date."

For a lot of people, including Heidi, kisses aren't just an expression of how you're feeling—they're also a useful tool. The guy probably does want to kiss you. So Heidi thinks that if you go too fast, he'll lose interest. Every girl knows that one way to avoid that is not kissing on the first date—you've got to hold the prize out a little longer. Heidi thinks that's way too obvious: "I don't want to be like every other girl. I want to be a unique challenge, which is why I don't kiss on the second date. If the guy gets nothing, and he still comes back for a third date, that's when you know you've really got him on the hook."

But even Heidi hasn't always followed her own rule: "I kissed Spencer the very first time we went out. That's just where I was in my life at the time. It didn't scare Spencer away or cause him never to call me again, but it was still a mistake. It sent him the wrong message."

"Spencer and I stopped talking for a few months, and then he asked me out again. This time, I wanted things to go differently, so I acted differently. The next time he took me out, I didn't kiss him. And on our next date, I was strong again. When we went out a third time, I didn't have to wonder what his motives were. I was confident that he wanted me and he wanted to get serious. He wasn't just another guy looking for one night of fun."

"Believe me, it's not easy to wait when you're genuinely attracted to someone," says Heidi, "but you have to set the tone. You have to show that you're worth working for and worth waiting for. The longer you can make him wait, the better. It might be hard for the first two dates, but every date after that will be so much better."

WHITNEY'S KISSING WISDOM

While Heidi has rules she could write out on a white-board and post in a classroom, Whitney is a little more flexible: "My rule is that I don't have a rule."

"I don't tend to kiss unless I really like a guy," says Whitney, "but I tend to know if I really like a guy right away. I don't have any sort of rule that says, 'I can do this on a second date, but I never do that on a first date.' If I'm feeling a kiss, the guy's going to get a kiss."

So what does Whitney say to people who insist that kissing a boy on the first date breaks the dating "rules"? "I think rules are for people who can't make decisions for themselves. What's the fun in life if you know everything you're going to do before you do it? It's fun to surprise someone now and then. Every once in a while, it can be fun to surprise yourself." Some-times, just listening to your instincts can tell you what you need to do—instead of following some rulebook in your head. Don't worry about all the labels people pin on girls depending on what they do and don't do with guys. You know what's best for you. But, if you're in doubt, Whitney recommends proceeding with cau-tion:

"Overall, I think it probably is better to go too slow rather than too fast. If you're not one hundred percent sure, don't rush things. You can always make up for lost time, but you can't unkiss a boy."

Whitney doesn't have a rule for kissing, but she does have boundaries: "If a guy is very, very lucky, he gets a kiss—but that's *all* he gets. You want a guy who will put a little bit of effort in, so he can't get *too* lucky right away. Think about it: if you won the lottery, you'd quit your job and you wouldn't work anymore. You don't want your guy to stop working for you, so don't let him win the lottery on the first night!"

A KISS IS JUST A KISS TO AUDRINA

For Audrina, kissing is really not that big of a deal: "A first-date kiss doesn't hurt a thing."

Girls need to relax about kissing on the first date. "If you feel like there's something there, one kiss isn't going to ruin anything," Audrina says. "I've certainly done it, and I never felt like it was a bad move."

But—there's kissing, and then there's, well, more

than kissing. The line has to be clearly drawn. "Anything *more* than a kiss is definitely a mistake. You really don't know a guy after one date, so you shouldn't rush things. Besides, no matter what they say, guys do lose interest when they get too much too fast."

Audrina believes that "guys should feel *lucky* to get a kiss on the first date. If they're not satisfied with that, that should tell you something about the guy. A guy who's too desperate on a first date may not be in it for the long haul. But if you find a guy with a little patience, he might be worth hanging on to."

Lauren's No-Kiss Plan

* *

Maybe you've decided you're going to be a "no-kiss" first dater. You're in good company—so is Lauren. This isn't easy in Los Angeles, where a lot of girls do more than kiss. But Lauren has invented a system called the No-Kiss Plan, guaranteed to take the awkwardness out of the end of that first date.

Most guys are pretty good at sensing when you want to be kissed, so if you're not interested, don't send out that vibe. Don't touch his shoulder or his arm, don't gaze into his eyes, and stay out of the "kiss zone" (the three-foot circle around both of your faces).

But if he still doesn't get it and insists on going in for it, there's an easy way to tell him no without actually telling him "No."

HOW LAUREN CONQUERS THE NO KISS

Lauren is definitely the organized type, so leave it to her to have a whole plan in place to ward off unwanted male lips. "I rarely kiss on the first date," she says, "so I had to come up with a 'no kiss' strategy."

First, Lauren evaluates the situation. "If I really like a guy, I'll hold his hand on the first date. I do this mostly as a test: I won't kiss a guy who won't hold my hand. If he's embarrassed to show me a little affection in public, I'm not going to show him affection in private. If he's comfortable and cool with it, he may get a kiss on the second date."

But that still leaves the problem of the first date. As a "no-kiss" dater in L.A., Lauren finds herself in an uncomfortable position at the end of virtually every first date. "There aren't a lot of 'no kiss' guys in L.A.," she says.

Even so, Lauren sticks to her plan. She sends clear signals. "The end of the first date is always awkward, because no one knows what the other person is thinking. Usually, guys are pretty good at picking up your vibe, but there are things you can do to help send a hint. I always carry a lot of lip gloss, and as we're pulling into my driveway, I'll put on a nice, thick coat. The guy gets the idea that if he wants to kiss me, he'll soon be wearing a nice, thick coat of lip gloss himself."

But if the guy is particularly persistent, he might still go for the mouth. So Lauren has developed a foolproof backup to the no-kiss strategy. This one will thwart even the most determined smacker.

STEP ONE: THE PIVOT Wait until the last second, then subtly turn your head a few degrees. His kiss will land on your cheek, not your lips. Just be careful not to swivel too soon, or you'll give him a chance to swivel with you.

STEP TWO: THE SELL Smile and act like it's nothing weird. You need to convince him that a peck on the cheek is what you were expecting all along.

STEP THREE: THE HUG AND HOP Don't give him a chance to try again. Give him a quick hug, then hop out of the car.

Before he knows what's hit him, you'll be safely inside your house with the door shut.

How to Get through the All-Important First Kiss

1. Get it out of the way before that so-awkward end-of-the-night moment. If you're doing the kissing, try to keep it spontaneous. Pick some moment when you're both laughing or looking at each other and just lean over.

2. Keep it short and tongueless. Just a nice soft peck on the lips will do for the very first kiss. You can get into the tongue wrestling on the second kiss.

3. Don't feel the need to start chattering about nothing the minute the kiss is over, and try to resist the requisite nervous giggle. It's okay if there's a little pause or silence. At the same time, don't worry if one or both of you say something lame or awkward. It happens, and after the second kiss, you won't feel so weird.

4. Try not to obsess over details such as eyes open or closed? Pucker or no pucker? What should I do with my hands? Believe me, he's going to be so glad to get a kiss from you that he won't be thinking about any of these things either.

• • • •

Someone Must Pay!

• •

You had filet. He had lobster tail. You both had wine and dessert. You can only imagine what this bill is going to come to. So what happens when the waiter sets that black leather folder on the table? Do you both lunge for it? Or do you sit back and scrape up that last bit of chocolate mousse while he roots around for his wallet?

Besides the good-night kiss, taking care of the bill is the most awkward part of a date. Here are a few ways to handle it without embarrassing your guy or going broke.

HOW TO HANDLE THE BILL LIKE AN AUDRINA

Audrina's not exactly an old-fashioned girl, but she does follow tradition. "I let the guy pay on the first date," she says. "I'll offer to pay on the second, third, or fourth date, but I think it's a little weird if the guy isn't all over the check on the first."

"On the second date, I usually try to pay for some part of the night. Maybe I'll let the guy get dinner, but I'll pick up the movie. I make my own money, so it shouldn't always fall on the guy to pay for everything. Plus, it's a good way to show the guy that you're interested. You're not just in it for a free meal!" You can also offer to put down the tip if he picks up the bill. Or buy him coffee or a drink if you go somewhere afterward.

According to Audrina, the worst thing a guy can do is to try to impress her with money he doesn't have.

"I've dated a lot of starving artists, and I have nothing against simple dates, but guys should know to choose a place they can afford. Don't go big if you can't back it up." If a guy's budget is strictly pizza and beer, that's cool. But he needs to own it—not pretend he's really more of an Ivy kind of guy.

There's overspending—and then there's just plain rudeness. Audrina recalls a double date she and Lauren went on with a couple of models. "We went to Area, and as soon as we got into the club, the guys were talking to the VIP hostess about getting a table and bottle service. Lauren and I would have been fine getting a couple of drinks at the bar, but these guys wanted to act like big shots . . . until the bill came. As soon as the waitress laid down the check, one guy walked away and the other just turned his back! The waitress just stood there waiting for money. Lauren and I were so embarrassed, so I ended up putting the whole thing on my credit card just to stop the awkwardness. Our first date was also our last date." There's a word for that kind of behavior: freeloading.

Audrina says it's not the money but the idea that bothered her: "If we had gone out a few times and I knew the guy I was with better, I would have been happy to pay. If it was our third or fourth date and I liked the guy, I probably would have even offered to pay. I don't expect the guy to pick up the bill every time, but I also don't expect him to put us both in an awkward situation. When it's time to pay, I love to offer, but I hate to be forced."

HOW TO HANDLE FIRST DATES LIKE A HEIDI

According to Heidi, girls need to have standards: "I never pay on the first date. I don't even bring my wallet."

But Heidi feels that this can change as time goes

on: "When you get more comfortable, you can offer to pay once in a while if you feel like it, but in the early stages, it's the man's responsibility to pay, one hundred percent of the time." In Heidi's world, guys and girls are actually both shelling out for the date—it's just that the girls do all the paying beforehand.

"It may not seem fair that guys have to pay for so much of dating, but it's cheaper than being a girl," Heidi explains. "A guy can look good in jeans and sneakers. We girls have to try a little harder, and it doesn't come cheap. When I go on a date, I always try to look my absolute best, which means a trip to the hair salon, a manicure/pedicure, a facial, professional makeup, a new dress, and usually new shoes to match that new dress. Even if the guy treats you to steak and champagne, he's getting off easy."

Heidi believes this is all just part of being a girl. Girls spend money on looking good, and boys spend money on good-looking girls—that's the deal. "A lot of times I'll go to a club or a bar with only my ID, because I know someone will have a bottle or offer to buy me drinks. That's why I don't bother lugging my purse around."

"You should never pay your own way," Heidi concludes. "If you are paying your own way, you're doing something wrong."

Lo's Dating Woes

• •

Lo is the girl who always has something funny to say. Whether it's on the topic of boys, clothes, work, or dating, Lo is always there to add a little humor and, often, a little truth to any situation.

So far, there's been a lot of talk about what girls can do right on a date. Here, Lo turns it around and talks about what a boy can do wrong on a date. According to Lo, there's quite a bit that boys can—and often do—screw up.

Here's Lo's list of the worst *things a guy can do on a date.*

BAD SHOES START A DATE ON THE WRONG FOOT "Shoes are a huge issue," says Lo, "and tragically, a lot of boys have terrible taste in that department. Guys have to get the shoes right before they can get the rest of the date right."

"Hiking boots are a no, and brown loafers are a no. I just don't like them . . . unless they're Gucci."

"It's bad for boys to wear running shoes on a date.

The only time that running shoes are okay is if we're going to work out on the date," Lo says, thinking about it. "But if I have to work out on a date, then that's a bad date, so running shoes are never okay."

BORING BOYS TAKE GIRLS ON BORING DATES

"When a guy plans a night, it's his chance to show a girl that he's different, he's special, and he's unique," Lo says. "So why do so many guys choose the same boring date that every other boring guy in the world would choose? Picking a dull, uncreative date says two things about you: that you're dull and uncreative."

"Don't make a girl sit through a long, boring dinner on the first date. Unexpected, unconventional dates are always better. Bring a girl somewhere she's never been and never would have gone without you."

Lo sums this up into one very simple rule: "Never be boring!"

NICE IS NICE, BUT *TOO* NICE IS A TURNOFF

"Speaking of boring," says Lo, "there is such a thing as *too* nice. Every girl wants a guy who will treat them well, but most of all we want a guy who acts like a guy, not a butler. When a guy comes across as someone you could walk all over, girls lose interest right away."

Lo offers this advice: "Stand up for yourself, speak

your mind, and hold your ground. The guy who always speaks up and says what he wants will eventually get everything he wants without having to say anything."

CONVERSATION IS A DIALOGUE, NOT A MONO-LOGUE "This is another obvious one that guys repeatedly get wrong," Lo says. "Talk has to go two ways. We don't want you to sit there and talk about how great you are for three hours. We're smart—if you're cool, we'll figure it out on our own. And most cool people have something else to talk about other than how cool they are."

Lo says, "But on the other hand, a date shouldn't feel like an interview or an interrogation. Given the choice, most girls actually would rather talk about themselves than listen to some guy ramble on about himself. The evening should never become about one person. There has to be an in-between."

Lo sums it up like this: "Talking *and* listening are both important. A good date feels like a balance."

GIVE A GIRL A CHANCE TO MISS YOU "When a guy doesn't call, it's a deal breaker," Lo says. "But when a guy calls too soon, it's a major deal breaker. If you're always eager, you're never attractive."

"It's a simple rule, but a lot of guys have trouble

getting this right," Lo says. "Some guys still call you first thing the next morning after a date. Some will even call you that night!"

Lo devised her own little chart to help boys remember:

Texting or calling the night of the date = way too desperate.

Texting or calling the day after the date = a little too desperate for my taste.

Texting or calling the day after the day after the date = just right.

REELING HIM IN

Well, congratulations, lady, you made it through the first date. For a few dicey moments he started going on about his fascination with motocross, but you managed to head him off. You dazzled him with your sparkling wit, you looked great in your new Blue Cult jeans, and you blew him away with your dance-floor moves after dinner. That's it—he's officially hooked.

But before you throw on those old pj's and crawl under the covers for the night, don't forget that you've still got work to do. You thought you were done? Oh, honey, your work has only begun. *Just because you have him on your line doesn't guarantee you'll get him in your boat. Getting him to take the bait was just step one—now you have to reel him in.*

Here's everything you need to know to take things to the next level and turn that nice little catch in a real meal.

Dress the Part

• •

Of course, in an ideal world, you'd look perfect every single time you see your guy. He shows up unannounced to take you to the beach, and you just happen to answer the door in your adorable new cotton sundress, with your hair washed and perfectly tousled and just the right touch of berry lip gloss on your newly exfoliated lips. Yeah. Try the reality: answering the door with a mouthful of the cold pizza you were eating for breakfast, a greasy I'm-going-to-take-a-shower-one-of-these-days ponytail, and your SARA'S SWEET SIXTEEN *T-shirt with the hole right over the boob.*

So what? you might ask. I thought that clothes really aren't important—what matters is who you are on the inside, blah blah. Well, of course clothes really aren't that important. You know how boring those people who only talk about appearances are. But we can't deny that when you look good—whatever that means to you, jeans, evening gown, bathing suit, whatever—you often feel good. How you look affects how you feel, how you feel affects how you act, and how you act affects who you are. In that sense, yes, even though who you are on the inside is ultimately what counts, clothes are important.

Everyone talks about what to wear on date number one. Heidi tells us what to wear on date two through date two hundred and twenty-two.

HOW HEIDI FIGHTS THE FRUMP

Looking good for the longtime boyfriend can get old after a while. Even Heidi admits it: "Spencer and I have been dating for a long time, but I try to keep the spirit of the first date alive."

With the longtime boyfriend, you don't have the thrill of the chase to keep that adrenaline pumping. You've caught him, he's crazy about you, it's a done deal. Bring out the sweats! Not according to Heidi: "It's easy to get frumpy when you've been dating the same guy for a long time. You know he loves you, you know he's attracted to you, and you pretty much know how the date is going to end. Plus, he's already seen you at your cranky, exhausted worst, so sometimes it seems silly to try to present yourself as this perfect beauty."

You don't need to be someone you're not, ever, Heidi points out. "When you live with a guy, you don't want to wear high heels and makeup every second of your life, but you also don't want to let yourself go. Once you stop taking care of how you look, it's only a matter of time before you stop taking care of other aspects of your relationship." For instance, you could try wearing a tank top instead of that old T-shirt. Or yoga pants instead of the giant sweatpants you've had since eighth grade. Wash your hair. Wash your face. You get the idea.

That's not to say Heidi never dresses down: "There are times when I need to crash out in something cozy. And sometimes I want to wear something shocking that rattles him. I'm very big on lingerie, so whenever I can, I try to wear something nice to sleep. After all, the bedroom is just another place to look good!"

Boys Know Boys

• •

Is it too much of a cliché to say that it's hard to know what's going on inside a guy's head? Oh, well, we're going to say it anyway. After all, half the time, guys don't even know what's going on inside their own heads.

Homo masculinius, the human male, can be a diffi-cult species to understand. His behavior is unpredictable, his words are few and vague, and while one has to assume he does in fact think, it's never clear exactly what he's thinking about.

But unless you are an anthropologist or a psychic, you're going to have to come up with a strategy for under-standing boys, interpreting their speech, and predicting their behavior, if you're going to be with one for the long haul. Here's how Audrina attempts to get inside the male mind.

HOW AUDRINA TRANSLATES GUY TALK

When Audrina has boy questions, she always goes straight to the source. "If you want guy advice," Audrina says, "just ask a guy."

And the best guys to ask? The ones you're definitely *not* dating—such as your brother, cousins, or best friends from growing up. They have no reason to give you anything but the straight truth. This is what Audrina does: "I come from a tight-knit family, so I always have guys around to give me advice. I go to my brother, Mark, a lot when I want to know how a guy thinks, or what a guy would do. If I'm writing an e-mail or a text, I'll ask Mark to help me write it. Sometimes I'll even have Mark write it for me." Sounds good, Audrina. Just make sure you read it beforehand. You never know when Mark might decide to get back at you for that orange slushie incident in fifth grade.

Audrina remembers one time when she was having trouble with Justin: "He kept disappearing, and he wouldn't answer my texts. Mark grabbed my phone and started typing away. Justin called me one minute later! I still don't know what Mark wrote, but it definitely got Justin's attention."

"When Mark's not around, I'll even ask my dad," Audrina says. "It's a little weird talking to your father about the boys you're dating, but he has really good advice." Strange as it may seem, dads were actually young once too. And even though we like to flatter ourselves that we're sooo different from our parents, the truth is that guys and girls have basically been after

Your *HILLS* Identity

In case you still haven't figured it out, here's your second chance at determining which Hills *girl you really are.*

1. Your companions for a perfect night out would be:
   (a) A small group of your closest girlfriends
   (b) Just you and your best friend
   (c) A big group of the rowdiest types you can collect
   (d) Everyone at the club

2. On a date, you'd most likely wear:
   (a) A sundress
   (b) A linen sheath
   (c) A black tank top and jeans
   (d) White ruffles

3. Your favorite movie is:
   (a) *Dirty Dancing*
   (b) *Breakfast at Tiffany's*
   (c) *Rebel Without a Cause*
   (d) *How to Lose a Guy in 10 Days*

4. Your iPod playlist consists mostly of:
   (a) A balanced mixture of new pop and rock and old favorites from your childhood
   (b) Classical music and folk ballads
   (c) Indie rock and punk
   (d) Whatever is newest on the pop charts
5. Your favorite shoes are most likely:
   (a) Classic ballet flats
   (b) Peep-toe pumps
   (c) Motorcycle boots
   (d) Your three-inch stilettos

IF YOU *answered mostly (a), you're a Lauren: balanced, understated, and serious, though you definitely know how to have fun. If you answered mostly (b), you're a Whitney: elegant, refined, and classy. If you answered mostly (c), you're an Audrina: rebellious, independent, and alternative. If you answered mostly (d), you're a Heidi: carefree, feminine, and flirty.*

the same things since the beginning of time. So your dad, assuming he's a cool guy, is always a good bet.

"Whether it's my family, my Epic coworkers, or just good male friends, I always have a good group of guys around that I can go to for advice. Guys are complicated, and it's too hard trying to figure out what they're thinking. It's just much easier to ask a guy."

So if you're having trouble understanding your guy, just find a guy who understands you and ask him to translate. After all, it takes one to know one.

Dating Is a Marathon, Not a Sprint!

Oh, those heady days of meeting a new guy. You're up every night and sleeping half the day. The rest of your waking hours are spent picking out your outfit for that night's new adventure, and checking your phone a thousand times to see if he's called. But let's be honest. This is not real life. Eventually, much as we hate to say it, you're going to have to come back down to earth—you know, work, school, taking out the garbage, scrubbing your sink, all of those things?

Eventually, the all-night talk marathons and spur-of-the-moment trips out of town are going to turn into on-the-couch DVD dates and joint trips to the grocery store. So how do you keep the romance alive when you're arguing about different brands of turkey breast?

Heidi talks about how she switched gears when she wanted to go from being the crazy player to the serious girlfriend.

HOW TO GO THE DISTANCE LIKE A HEIDI

"Going fast can be fun sometimes," says Heidi, "but going fast is always a mistake." Ever heard of crash and burn? Well, it's a lot easier to crash when you're traveling at a dangerous speed.

"In a lot of ways, I have a guy's mentality when it comes to dating," Heidi says. "I'm confident, I'm impatient, and I say whatever's on the tip of my tongue. I'm basically like a cocky guy."

Heidi's not denying that moving fast has its advantages: "When you're on the offensive, it means never waiting around for the phone to ring—if you want to talk to a guy, you call him right up. You never wait for a cute guy to say hello—you walk straight across the bar and start talking to him. You never wait for anything, because you're always in fast-forward. It's really fun and it's really exciting . . . unless you actually like the guy."

"But," Heidi warns, "when real emotion comes into it, the game changes. It's one thing to be the girl running around the club, talking to a million boys. But when you're actually thinking about one boy, the running around leaves you empty." Sometimes, though, you have to do a little running around. Trying different ways of meeting guys can help you figure out what you really want.

"When I started having real feelings for Spencer, I suddenly didn't care about being the girl who would say anything to anybody anytime. I only wanted to be with Spencer, all the time. But it can be hard to convince someone that you can be a serious girlfriend if they've only seen you as a serious flirt."

Heidi wouldn't trade her single days, if only for the lessons they taught her: "When I look back at how I used to be, I think of it as the exact way *not* to date. I was doing everything a million miles an hour, but now I take things slow. I kept everything fun and light and silly and meaningless, but now I want meaning in my relationships. And I don't make a game of how many boys I can flirt with in one night. I want to be with the same boy, each and every night."

"If you ever want a serious relationship, being a player only hurts you. So I'm glad my player days are behind me," Heidi says, "but they were definitely fun while they lasted!"

Boyfriend Patrol

Now for an unpleasant truth that may come as a shock to some of the more innocent types reading this: boys aren't perfect. Try not to fall out of your chair. And one of the ways their perfection is lacking is that sometimes, only sometimes, they can "forget" that an exclusive relationship is just that—exclusive.

Of course, you can do many things to keep your boyfriend from straying: buy a leash, hire a private detective, or have yourself surgically sewn to his body. But short of stalking (and who wants to be a stalker?) all you can really do is make sure he understands the exact meaning of "do not cheat." Depending on your guy, you might have to do some remedial training.

But sometimes the biggest threat to your relationship isn't that your boyfriend will want to cheat with another girl, it's that one of your best friends (sorry, supposed best friends) wants to cheat with your boyfriend. Unfortunately, the very people who are supposed to be watching your back are sometimes the same people who stab you there.

None of us want to live in a world without friends, and we can't be suspicious 100 percent of the time. But you have to know that betrayal comes from those close to us as often as it comes from far away.

The sad truth is that when it comes to relationships, friends can be your worst enemies.

HOW TO BE LOYAL LIKE A LAUREN

Lauren definitely knows right from wrong, and she's not afraid to say it: "There's definitely a code among girls. You don't get together with your friends' exes, no matter how casual or long ago it was."

Lauren had an unfortunate situation come between her and Jen Bunney, one of her best and oldest friends from Laguna Beach. "We grew up together in Laguna Beach," Lauren remembers. "I'd known her for fifteen years, and I was happy to have her in Los Angeles with me. There are a lot of phony people in

L.A., and it's hard to tell the people who care about you from the people who only care about themselves. With Jen Bunney, I didn't have to worry about that . . . at least, that's what I thought."

That all changed when Lauren took Jen out to celebrate Jen's twenty-first birthday at Geisha House and Les Deux. "I wanted to do something nice to show her just how good a friend she had been, so I gave her a diamond necklace. I'm not much of a toast maker, but at dinner I raised a glass and said, 'To Jen, one of my oldest friends, who's *always* been there for me.'" Lauren didn't know it then, but that night their fifteen-year relationship was about to be destroyed in fifteen minutes.

"The trouble came when we moved on to Les Deux and met up with Brody. I had been dating Brody on and off, and even though we were in one of our 'off' periods, I didn't expect him to be going after my friends. I *definitely* didn't expect my friends to be going after him." But while Lauren was overseeing the party and trying to make sure Jen had a good time, Jen ducked out and left the club with Brody.

As Lauren explains, "I really wasn't mad that Jen hooked up with Brody. At that point, I was over him, and I was starting to think of him more as a friend. If Jen had taken me aside and told me that she was starting to have feelings for Brody, I would have told her to go for it."

"I was really mad that Jen went behind my back. She knew it was shady, she knew it would hurt my feelings, and she did it anyway. Certainly, there were other people to blame as well, but she tried to make me look like an idiot, and that's just really painful coming from a friend. In the end, the worst thing to come out of that night was the damage it did to my relationship with Jen, not my relationship with Brody."

"When it comes to friends, it's just not worth it to mess around," Lauren says. "No boy is worth losing a friend over. Good friends are just too valuable to risk."

HOW AUDRINA LEARNED A LIFE LESSON

Audrina may be the rebellious type, but she just won't cross certain lines—and messing around with a friend's boyfriend is one of them. "Anyone can let you down," she says, "but your best friends can let you down the most."

Audrina's first high school boyfriend was a guy named Dan: "He was too old for me, he was covered head to toe in tattoos, and my parents couldn't stand him. I was in love."

"Not only did I have a boyfriend that I was nuts about, but I had two best friends that I loved and trusted. Everything in my life was perfect, until I found out that my boyfriend was cheating on me . . . with my two best friends."

Audrina never expected to be betrayed by two people she thought she could trust: "How could something like that happen right in front of my face? I was young and naïve, and I didn't have my guard up. My parents told me Dan was trouble, but I didn't want to hear it. Most of all, I didn't want to believe that two girls who were supposed to be my friends could do something like that to me. If you can't trust your best friends, who can you trust?"

For years, Audrina couldn't understand how two girls who were so nice to her face could do something so awful behind her back. But a lot of times when people do terrible things, it's much more about them than it is about you. And this was the case with one of these girls. One day, Audrina got a letter from her.

"She had gone through some tough times," Audrina remembers reading. "Now, she was getting

help and she was apologizing to everyone she had screwed over."

"She said that she always felt competitive with me. She was jealous of how happy I was with my boyfriend, and she wanted to prove to herself that she was on my level. Her twisted way of doing that was to sleep with my boyfriend. She said that she needed to do it to feel good about herself. Of course, all it proved was that she was way *below* my level, because I don't need to go around stealing other people's men."

Even after the betrayal, Audrina remains positive about people and chooses to trust them: "Luckily, not all girls are like this! Now I have friends like Lauren who have too much respect for me and for themselves to go behind my back. But I still keep my guard up. For every loyal, trustworthy girl, there's a jealous back-stabber who wants to knock you down and raise herself up." Cheating hurts more when a friend commits the crime than a stranger. You trust your friends and have built up relationships with them. When someone betrays you, you wind up reevaluating yourself and your own judgment as well as theirs.

Random girls can be mean, but remember, your best friends can be vicious.

A Tale of Two Heidis

Why get one girl when you can get two for the price of one? At least, that's what Spencer got when he started dating Heidi—and her two personalities.

There is Heidi the Fun Party Girl, who bounced around every club in Hollywood, doing whatever she wanted. But just mention the word commitment *and you'd see her blond ponytail disappearing out the door. Then there's Heidi the Serious Girlfriend, who puts everything she has into her relationship.*

Here's how Heidi transformed herself from a career player to a full-time girlfriend.

HOW HEIDI UPGRADED TO 2.0

"Spencer dated the old Heidi before he dated the new and improved," Heidi says. "He got the rest of me before he got the best of me."

Not everyone knows this, but Heidi and Spencer had a brief fling before starting their serious relationship. "This is actually the second time Spencer and I have dated," Heidi says. "We dated briefly a couple of years ago, while I was in full-on 'player' mode. I was out every night, going a million miles an hour, doing whatever I wanted, whenever I felt like it. Obviously, that didn't end well."

But things weren't working the way Heidi wanted them to when she was in player mode, so she changed things up. She downshifted and started taking things slow. She let Spencer know that if he was interested in her, he'd have to do the pursuing, he'd have to wait a little while, and most of all, he'd have to work.

Heidi recalls, "I basically became a whole new Heidi. Old Heidi would call Spencer whenever she felt like seeing or talking to him. New Heidi changed her phone number. Spencer had to find the number on his own."

"Old Heidi let Spencer know that he was one of

many boys she was talking to. New Heidi let Spencer know that he was the only boy she was talking to, so if he wanted to stick around, New Heidi better be the only girl he's even *thinking* about."

"Old Heidi kissed Spencer on the first date. New Heidi didn't kiss on the first *or* the second date. (Remember, this is New Heidi we're talking about. Spencer had never been out with New Heidi before, so it was technically a first date.)

"Now, Spencer has dated both Heidis," she says, "and he's definitely happier with New Heidi. Guys love a challenge, and they like to know that they've earned the very best of you. Spencer knows there are a million girls running around at clubs, but none of them will

give him what he gets from the relationship we've built and invested in."

Most important, Heidi is happier with the New Heidi. "I'm proud that I know how to be a good girl-friend, proud of all the work I've put into my relation-ship with Spencer, and proud of all the work I've put into me. New Heidi is supportive, New Heidi is atten-tive, and New Heidi shares her feelings. Old Heidi definitely never did that!"

Keeping Him Interested

You met a great guy. He asked you out. The first date led to a second. The second date led to a toothbrush at his place. Now you haven't slept in your own bed in a month, you've coordinated your TiVo schedules, and he actually stayed awake during Sweet Home Alabama *last weekend.*

The hard part is over, right? Wrong!

This is the same guy who watches six TV channels at once. He talks on the phone and texts while driving. Video games and YouTube have whittled his attention span down to that of an eight-year-old. So how do you expect Mr. ADD to stay interested in you for the rest of his life?

Getting a boyfriend is one thing. Hanging on to one re-quires a different set of skills altogether.

AUDRINA ADVISES, "DON'T LET YOUR ROMANCE RUIN HIS 'BROMANCE'"

Audrina understands the unique relationship that your boyfriend has with his buddies: "Best friends are more than friends. They're like brothers."

"His other friends are just guys to watch sports and brag about girls with," Audrina explains, "but his best friend sticks up for him, helps him through tough times, and keeps his most personal secrets. This is a deep, lasting, meaningful relationship that comes close to romance. I call it a bromance." His "bromantic" buddy is the one he climbed Mount Washington with. Even though their entire conversation seems to consist only of grunts, your guy seems happier after he's been hanging out with his best friend. They doubled-dated at senior prom and pulled a string of pranks on each other when they lived together during college. This is a sacred relationship, so take this word from the wise: don't mess with it if you want any chance of hanging on to your guy.

Audrina warns, "If your boyfriend's best friend doesn't like you, you won't be around for long. I've seen it a thousand times. Never mind that you and your boyfriend are totally happy. Best friends can find a way to convince their buddy that you're no good for him."

"Sometimes, you might not be able to figure out why the best friend doesn't like you. You've been nothing but nice, but still he acts mean and makes you feel unwelcome. The best friend may not even know why he's doing this, but it's simple: he's jealous and threatened by you. Things were great before you got there, but now he thinks you're going to come between them. You're going to spoil the bromance."

"The best friend is afraid that you're going to make your boyfriend dress differently, talk differently, and act differently," Audrina explains. "He thinks you're going to ruin the guy he already thinks is perfect. Or he might be afraid that you're going to cut way back on your boyfriend's 'guy time' and steal him away altogether." You need to show the friend that you're not the least bit interested in breaking up the bromance. Don't try to horn in on their guy time together—poker night does not include the new girlfriend. When you're around the friend, don't treat him like an annoying tagalong brother—talk to him. Get him to tell you funny stories about your new guy. Tell him things about yourself so that *he* can see you as a person too. Find a subtle way to tell the friend how cool it is that the two of them have such a strong bond—and that you're going to respect that."

Audrina agrees, "The way to get in with the best friend is to show him that you like your boyfriend for exactly who he is, and that you're not trying to change him. Show him that you respect their friendship, and you wouldn't do anything to get in the way of it. The best friend will realize that you both want the same thing: for your boyfriend to be happy. His bromance will stay strong, but your romance will grow even stronger."

Keep Small Problems Small

* *

Haven't we all been in this situation? You and your boyfriend are at dinner. You're not having a great day, and so when he says, "Is that your second piece of chocolate cake?" you immediately burst into tears.

"Haven't I told you not to call me fat?" you scream.

He glares. "I wasn't calling you fat. I was just saying—"

"I know what you were saying!" you respond through your tears. "You were saying my butt looks like Alaska!"

Okay, so maybe he had forgotten that you don't like it when he comments on your food. And maybe you were feeling just a tad oversensitive that night. But it's just a small problem, right? Well . . . yeah. But small problems can grow into big problems if you let them build up without dealing with them.

Most people ignore relationship problems, hoping that they'll go away on their own. Heidi has learned the hard way that you have to deal with the little issues before they get out of hand. Even if it leads to a few more fights in the long run, they'll be smaller fights, and when they're over, they'll be over.

No one enjoys fighting with their loved one, but the truth is it's part of any relationship. So if you have to fight, fight smart, and get yourself into the habit of fighting fair.

HOW HEIDI KNOWS WHAT'S WORTH FIGHTING FOR

"You have to talk about problems the moment they come up," Heidi believes, "and then never, ever, bring it up again."

Heidi's mom has some good advice: "My mother always told me that when things are going wrong, look at yourself first." Heidi says, "That's why I'm always the first to apologize. I avoid a lot of blowups and fights that way. But every once in a while, every couple disagrees. When that happens, we make a point of dealing with it then and there. Our goal is to address it, fix it, and then move on with our happy lives. I don't go to bed angry, and I never bottle things up."

"Usually, when you have a huge fight over a tiny thing, it's not really about that tiny thing at all. It's about something bigger that happened a long time ago, and you and your boyfriend didn't put in the effort to deal with it at the time. It's been bottled up and growing, and now it's become a very big, very real problem." Take the chocolate cake example from earlier. Maybe the real issue is that you feel as if he's always criticizing you. And maybe he is. Either way, that's a much bigger issue than whether you're getting fat. So, if it's possible, try to not freak out when he makes an (admittedly) obnoxious comment like the one about two pieces of cake. Instead, if you can, take a deep breath and say something like "I feel like you're being really critical of me. This seems to happen a lot and it makes me feel awful." If you can get this out in a calm voice, so much the better. He might be mad at first, but you'll have said what you need to say. Later, you can talk about it more.

Heidi believes that there's a right way and a wrong way to argue: "When we fight, I try to stay calm. I don't raise my voice. I do my best to look at it from Spencer's point of view. Spencer is not afraid to talk about his feelings, so every problem can be talked out, if we keep our heads. I remind myself that Spencer and I are both rational adults, so there must be a rational, adult solution to whatever problem we're having."

"When we're fighting, I prevent myself from dredging up the past," Heidi says. "I only talk about the issue we're dealing with at that very moment. It helps us stay focused on the actual problem, and it forces us to speak very openly about our feelings on this specific topic, rather than turning it into this big, general complaint. Small, specific problems are easy to solve. Big, general complaints are impossible to solve. Staying in the present helps small fights stay small."

Friends Will Always Come First

It's easy to get caught up in a new relationship. You're spending more and more time with your new boyfriend, and it's natural that you don't have time for a few of the things you used to do.

Maybe first you miss your weekly brunch with the girls. Next, you bail on a good friend's birthday party because your guy just got Fall Out Boy *tickets. Your girlfriends come over for the weekly movie night you forgot to cancel, and whoops! you're cuddled on the couch with your new guy, watching* Iron Man. *All of a sudden, you haven't hung out with your girlfriends for two months, and they've forgotten what you look like.*

Nothing is quite as much fun as the first few months of a new relationship, but it's important to remember the people who have always been there for you. Keep in mind, if the relationship goes south, who's going to bring over the pints of Ben & Jerry's and Dirty Dancing? *Not your ex, that's for sure.*

Audrina believes in the importance of keeping good people in your life and does her best to balance friendship and romance.

HOW TO HOLD ON TO FRIENDS LIKE AN AUDRINA

"Guys may come and go," Audrina says, "but they usually go."

Audrina believes that no romance is worth ending a friendship over: "I've made my share of mistakes

when it comes to guys, but one thing I am proud of is I've always held on to my friends. My friends are honest, they're reliable, and they don't judge me. That's more than I can say about most guys, so I never cut my friends out. They're just too valuable."

Only so many hours are in a day, so most people struggle with finding time for friends and boyfriends. Audrina solves this by combining those times: "I usually bring my girlfriends around when I'm going to meet a guy. This way, I get to spend time with both of them, and they both get to meet someone who's important to me. A good friend or a good boyfriend should want to get to know the people in my life." Vice versa works also. When Audrina, Lauren, and Lo went to Vegas to surprise Brody on his birthday, Audrina brought Justin along, even though he was the only guy in their group.

Audrina knows that this strategy doesn't work for everyone: "Lauren is more serious about being with people, and she prefers one-on-one time when she's dating someone. Alone time is important, and I respect that, but it just makes it harder to make time for everyone else. It means you have to set aside another night for just your girlfriends." You can also get creative with how you share your evenings. Make dinner plans with your girls, for instance, but then tell your guy you'll meet him for drinks later. Or if you know you'll be seeing your guy on Saturday night, then plan to spend Saturday afternoon with your girlfriends.

The other cardinal rule to maintaining friendships is that you've got to be there in times of crisis. When you pick up the phone and all you hear on the other end is sobbing, be ready to cancel your guy plans. Audrina's had personal experience with this one: "No guy likes to be canceled on, but if he really likes you, he'll put up with it. The other day I was invited to a barbecue by this Australian BMX rider named Corey. I really wanted to go, but I got a call from my friend Sky, and she was having a bad day. She would never ask me to cancel my plans, but she's a friend who has been there for me since high school, and I wasn't going to bail on her now."

"I called Corey and told him I'd have to see him another time. I knew he'd be mad, and at first he was. But eventually, he understood why I had to be there for my friend, and hopefully, he respects me for it. I know I wouldn't want to be with a guy who always lets his friends down, even if he was doing it to spend time with me."

Growing Up Together

It's easy to have a good relationship when everything is going great. When trouble comes up, then couples find out just how strong they really are. Maybe you're out for a hike and your guy sees a giant hill he decides he wants to climb. But there are huge NO CLIMBING signs everywhere. He wants to take the risk; you think he's being an idiot. He ignores you and leaves you back on the trail sitting on a rock while he goes off and climbs the hill. You punish him by giving him the silent treatment the rest of the way home.

So what should you do to restore harmony? You're going to have to talk about it, preferably without yelling or

Guys and the Phone: The Basics

· · · · · · · · · · · · · · · · ·

Lesson 1: Guys generally consider the phone simply a tool to make plans. It is not a confessional or a tell-all hotline. If you want to have a successful conversation with a guy on the phone, you'd better have something concrete to say when he picks up.

Lesson 2: You know how seven dog years are like one human year? Same thing with the phone: ten minutes to a girl is like three hours to a guy. Keep it short.

Lesson 3: Do not, under any circumstances, even if you're in Japan and he's in Mexico, try to discuss feelings, emotions, or touchy relationship subjects on the phone with a guy. You will get nothing but a lot of heavy silences. Whatever it is, it can wait until you can look him in the eye.

Lesson 4: If he's either at work or out with his buddies when you call, don't torture him by making him respond to little cute lines like "I love you. Do you love me?" All you'll get is a mumbled "Yeah" in response, so don't waste your time.

· · ·

accusations. How *you discuss problems that arise says a lot about both the kind of couple you are and what kind of future you might have.*

Here's how Heidi anticipates the imperfect moments and looks on them as an opportunity to make her relationships stronger.

HOW HEIDI EMBRACES HER MISTAKES

Heidi says she doesn't stress when she or Spencer makes a mistake in their relationship. If you're realistic, then the pressure's off—it's not just likely that you and your boyfriend are going to make a few missteps along the way, it's 100 percent certain. Anyone who says that she and her boyfriend don't fight is either lying, delusional, or just hasn't been going out long enough.

As Heidi puts it, "Choosing a boyfriend is choosing who you're going to make your mistakes with. You're always going to make mistakes, so of course your boyfriend is too. No one is ever going to be perfect. You're both going to screw up, because that's just a natural part of growing and learning and maturing in a relationship. If you know that going in, it takes a ton of pressure off of you and your boyfriend." So just accept that maybe what happened on the hike was a screwup, on both of your parts. He was probably being stubborn and dangerous by going off the trail, but that's up to him. You shouldn't have called him an idiot or given him the silent treatment—after all, he's entitled to break his own neck if he wants to. And he shouldn't have left you, his hiking partner, alone on the trail, just to follow a whim. You were hiking *together*, and he should have respected that.

Heidi offers this advice for girls about to get involved in serious relationships: "When you're choosing a boyfriend, don't go looking for a perfect person who's never going to do anything wrong. That guy doesn't exist. Find someone real who you want to grow up with. Find the person whose mistakes you can live with, and who will be supportive of you when you make mistakes."

BROKEN BOYFRIENDS

The 9-Guys

● ●

You've landed yourself a shiny new boyfriend. He doesn't even have training wheels, but he does have those nice little tassels that fly out from the handlebars when you ride really fast.

Things were amazing at first, then they settled down to okay. After that, things dropped to so-so, then slid to tolerable, then nose-dived to barely bearable, and finally plummeted to unacceptable. Your shiny new boyfriend isn't so shiny and new anymore. He's rusty and clanky and his chain is broken.

You're not quite ready to give up on your broken boy-friend, though, because you're pretty sure that with some oil and a tune-up, he can be fixed. But before you can start that work, you have to figure out exactly what's wrong with your boyfriend.

While guys can be wonderful in a lot of different ways, they tend to be bad in similar ways. Lauren, Whitney, Audrina, and Heidi have all run into their share of broken boyfriends, and Lauren has distilled them down into a group of boys she calls the I-Guys. Let's hope you can learn from the girls' mistakes.

So read on. You might find your broken boyfriend somewhere on this list.

THE SHY GUY

"This is the cute guy that you always see around," Lauren says. "You always say hi, you make every excuse to speak with him, but he never asks you out." He smiles at you, you smile at him, he smiles at you, you

smile at him—until the routine starts getting a little old. Short of burying him in little slips of paper with your number on them, he might never get the hint.

"Last year, there was this *really* cute busboy at Les Deux," Lauren says. "My friends and I would go, and we'd be approached by all these guys, but I'd be like, 'Get out of my way. I want to see the busboy.'"

"When we hung out, he always had a lot to say and we laughed a lot. But he never seemed to be able to get up the courage to come over on his own, so I always had to take the lead. At first, I used to make up excuses to talk to him. Then, I'd ask to be seated in the section where he was clearing dishes. By the end, I was intentionally spilling twelve-dollar cocktails, just so he'd have to come by and clean them up!" Obviously, there was only one solution for the Shy Guy busboy, if Lauren ever wanted to see him *not* holding a rag and carrying a stack of dirty dishes—ask him out!

Sometimes a Shy Guy can come out of his shell a little bit, but it's unlikely that he'll ever be a loud, brazen, take-charge type of guy. "Some guys are just born shy," Lauren says, "and there's nothing you can do to get them over it. But it gets a little tiresome always taking charge." So if you're not comfortable being in charge of all the plans and all the personality in the relationship, it may be time to say bye-bye to Shy Guy.

THE WHY? GUY

"Why? Guys are the leg warmers of men," Lauren says. "They seemed like a good idea at the time, but looking back, they're just embarrassing." Sometimes this is the effect of just taking off the beer goggles; sometimes you can blame it on the lighting. Either way, when you meet that guy who looked so good at the club a few nights before, you may find yourself wondering what attracted you to someone who talks with his mouth full and wears three earrings in one ear.

"This guy seemed so great in the dark club, but

he looks very different in the light of day," Lauren says. "Now you're wondering what you ever saw in him." Did he always chew like that? Did he always wear so much product in his hair? Did his jokes always suck? The answer to all those questions, unfortunately, is yes.

The Why? Guy shows you how powerful a first impression can be. "That one time that he seemed amazing forces you to second-guess the next five terrible dates he takes you on. You convince yourself that the diamond you saw on that first meeting is hiding somewhere inside the miserable lump of coal you're now at dinner with."

Have you ever met an amazing woman who has been married for years to the world's most boring man? Chances are, that husband is a Why? Guy, and the poor woman is *still* waiting for him to be the guy she thinks she saw when they first met. "Don't waste time waiting for a guy who bores you every day to suddenly thrill you again. The chances are, he was never that thrilling to begin with." People can change their clothes, career, and hair color, but that's about it. Otherwise, they tend to stay pretty much the same—for the rest of their lives. So don't hold your breath that the guy who likes Boggle now is suddenly going to transform into someone who likes windsurfing.

"Dating a guy you don't know very well is a little like making an impulse buy," Lauren explains. "Half the thrill is that you could be making a big mistake. Well, you just impulse-bought a sweater that doesn't look good, doesn't feel good, and clashes with everything you have. You can't take it back, so there's nothing left to do but throw it away."

THE LIE GUY

The Shy Guy and the Why? Guy might be unappealing, but they're probably still nice—unlike this next guy we're going to meet: the Lie Guy. "The Lie Guy always knows exactly what to say," Lauren explains. "Unfortunately, everything he says is a lie." The Lie Guy might be hot, confident, and give every appearance of being successful, but you'll never know because, if you're smart, you'll stop talking to him the minute you find out his true Lie Guy identity.

Lauren has met the Lie Guy several times in Hollywood: "Every word out of his mouth is exactly what you want to hear. He's filled with promises and praise, as well as alibis and excuses. He'll lie about his car, his job, his education—anything at all to make you interested."

"The scariest thing about the Lie Guy is that he's pathological. He lies because he *enjoys* it. They're wired differently than you and me, and they actually find pleasure in deceiving you. Deciding to be with a Lie Guy is signing up to spend the rest of your life sifting through a series of fibs, white lies, misdirects, and betrayals."

Of course, you're not going to have to worry about that because you're not going to be with a Lie Guy. Wouldn't you fire your doctor, your dog walker, or your mechanic if he lied to you? Of course you would—he's supposed to be on your side. Your boyfriend is supposed to be on your side too, so he deserves the same treatment. Fire the Lie Guy and find someone with enough respect for you, himself, and reality to tell the truth.

THE BI-GUY

"There are a lot of confused and experimental people out there," Lauren says. "Let's just say, there are some guys out there with some pretty surprising side interests." Gay guys can be the best friends a girl can have, but you're probably not going to have a lot of success on the romance front if your guy prefers other guys.

Lauren has an example from her own life: "I was set up on a date with a model once, and we ended up at Area. I ran into a good friend of mine who's openly gay, and I introduced him to my date. My gay friend looked at me like I was crazy. 'You're on a date with *him*? I used to go out with him.' This is one friend I never thought I'd be sharing dates with!" Lauren probably felt a little embarrassed by the situation, but most likely her date was blushing even harder.

So if you're dating a guy who repeatedly compliments your handbag, knows that your shoes are not only Prada but vintage Prada, refers to Kelly Clarkson as "Kel," and gets really excited about watching *Shakespeare in Love*, then tread carefully. You may just be dating a Bi-Guy. "Every girl dreams of meeting that guy with a great fashion sense, impeccable grooming, and who gets along with all your girl friends *really* well," Lauren says. "That guy definitely exists, but it may not be your dream scenario."

"There are a million reasons why that model was never going to be right for me, and I really don't care who he dated before me. Still, I would have appreciated it if he had been honest. I shouldn't have to hear things about a guy's past from other people."

How to Charm like Justin Bobby

Girls like mysterious men, and few men are more mysterious than Justin Bobby.

At first glance, Justin Bobby demonstrates some unusual behavior, and he may not fit the mold of the typical charmer. Then again, any guy who dates a girl like Audrina must be doing something right.

Perhaps no one can ever fully understand his methods, but here's one attempt to solve the riddle, wrapped in an enigma, shrouded in mystery, that is Justin Bobby.

1. Be Late
- Never be on time. You look too eager.
- Never be early. That's allowing someone else to waste your time.
- Keep things happening on your schedule. When you're late, everyone else is forced into your timeline.

2. Honk
- Set the tone early.
- You're not the type of guy who comes to the front door with roses; you're the type of guy who revs his El Camino in the driveway while lying on the horn.

- As long as your date has ears and legs, a honk is a fine way to kick off the evening.

3. Wear Disguises
- One day, be a dead ringer for Johnny Depp. The next day, dress like Eddie Vedder circa *Vitalogy*. The second people get used to your long hair, shave it all off and show up looking like Zorro without the mask.
- In a pinch, you can drape a sweatshirt over your head all night and wear it the way a Russian peasant woman would.

4. Never, Ever, Return Calls, Texts, or E-mails
- We live in a digital age, where people are constantly in communication. You live in the Stone Age, where someone is as likely to reach you by phone as they are by smoke signal.
- If being too available is a turnoff, ignoring all attempts at communication must be a huge turn-on. If someone is hoping to hear back from you this week, they'd better have left you a message in the late nineties.

5. Burp
- Loud and often.

6. Spin, Rock, Fidget, and Duck
- If you're on a barstool, spin it. If you're in a chair, rock back and forth like an asylum inmate. Fidget

with swizzle sticks. If there's nothing to fiddle with, just lay your head down on the table.
- The key is to stay in motion. It's harder to hit a moving target.

7. Bring Up Wildly Inappropriate Topics

- Whether on a date or meeting someone new, no topic is taboo. Nothing makes a first impression like discussing unbelievably delicate subjects with people you hardly know.
- Boobs? No problem!
- Drugs and alcohol? Why not?
- Sex toys? But of course.

8. Hit on Your Date's Best Friend

- It's difficult to explain why this works, it just does.
- Step one: get your date and her best friend in the same place.
- Step two: tell your date that you're only going out with her so that you can get to the best friend. Make sure that both the friend and best friend are present to hear it.
- Step three: sit back and enjoy the fireworks.

• • •

THE UNAVAILABLE GUY

All of the I-Guys are enticing, in their own ways (except for Lie Guy), but let's just admit it: no one is more desirable than the guy who breaks the mold— the Unavailable Guy. His label doesn't even rhyme with the others. Heidi is the first to admit, "Nothing makes me want something more than telling me I can't have it. What I have isn't enough—I want what she has, what he has, and what you have."

Picture this scenario: You're out with a group of friends and some guys wander over to join you. None of them seem particularly interesting, but you amuse yourself by chitchatting with the nondescript guy next to you. You're actually starting to get pretty bored, until a gorgeous, blond-haired girl wearing amazing black leather pants bounces over and perches herself on the lap of your chitchat buddy. They begin a massive PDA session and he completely tunes out to the world around him, including you. Turns out that black-leather-pants girl is his new honey. He can barely take his eyes off her for one second—and all of a sudden, he doesn't seem so nondescript anymore. Why didn't you notice before what sexy arms he has? And eyes. And hair, for that matter. Da-dum. It's happened: you've been taken by Unavailable Guy.

"Sometimes, not having something is the *only* reason I want it," Heidi says. "We girls like a good challenge, and we competitive girls *really* like a good challenge." That's the whole attraction of the Unavailable Guy.

"A married friend of mine told me that he never had more girls talk to him than when he started wearing a wedding band," Heidi says. "Think about how crazy that is: announcing to the world that he was already taken caused *more* girls to pursue him, not less."

Of course, going after guys in serious relationships is a complete waste of time: "You put all this time and energy into a guy, and when in the end you don't get him, you can't even complain to your friends. He was already taken, so why'd you waste your precious time on him in the first place?"

"But let's say he does leave his girlfriend or wife for you. Now you've intentionally started a relationship with a known cheater! And how can you be sure that he's a cheater? Because he cheated with you! A few months from now when you hear he's been messing around on you behind your back, you can't even act surprised."

"Don't get me wrong," Heidi says. "I still want it all. I want every promotion at work, I want every dress I see hanging in a boutique window, and every pair of killer boots I see walking down the street. But when I got serious with Spencer, I finally learned to appreciate what I have. I realized that there's nothing better out there, and I started taking pride in what I had, instead of driving myself crazy for what I didn't and could never have."

In the end, being happy with what you have is the only way to be happy, period. If you always want what you can't have, you'll never have what you want!

Bad Boys

* *

Oh, the Bad Boys. They're so annoying—always late, completely unreliable, and totally inappropriate in front of our parents. So why are they so irresistible? James Dean leaning against a brick wall with a cigarette dangling from his pouty lips has given way to baby-faced indie rockers in skinny jeans, but really, the Bad Boy has hardly changed since the days of Rebel Without a Cause—*heck, since the days of* Gone with the Wind. *Wasn't Rhett Butler the ultimate Bad Boy?*

Most girls (and women) can confess to succumbing to

a Bad Boy at some point in their love life. If we're honest with ourselves, we can admit that Bad Boys are like sky-diving, or traveling in the Amazon: they're exciting, they keep you guessing, they're fun, and they're a challenge. One of the classic reasons that girls stay with Bad Boys is that they think they can change him. "I'll be the one he gave up his Bad Boy ways for," they think.

Our girls have each had their turn with Bad Boys, with varying success. If you're going to go down this road your-self, try to learn from their good—and bad—experiences.

HOW TO HANDLE BAD BOYS LIKE A LAUREN

Take Lauren's advice—have fun with the Bad Boys. Just don't expect a marriage proposal—or an on-time date for dinner: "You'll be fine—as long as you have low ex-pectations."

"No one can disappoint you if you don't get your hopes up. It's only when you let yourself believe things are going to work out a certain way that you're let down," Lauren says. "The thing about Bad Boys is that they're easy to spot, and their reputation usually pre-

cedes them. If they always pull the same junk in all
their past relationships, don't expect them suddenly
to act completely different just because they're with
you. You need to know what you're getting into." Don't
let yourself fall into the he'll-change-for-me trap.
Trust us, every girl who has dated said Bad Boy before
you has thought the same thing—and now *you're* dating
him, which means their techniques obviously didn't
work. Bad Boys don't change. That's part of their mad-
dening Bad Boy appeal.

As Lauren puts it, "Every girl wants to be the girl
worth changing for, and every girl imagines she can
turn the Bad Boy into a good boyfriend. Some people
say you should find a guy who doesn't need changing,
but what's the fun in that? Who wants a perfect relationship? That's boring."

Lauren knows that while her advice is right, it's
not always the easiest thing to follow: "It's not like you
choose to be attracted to difficult guys with a history of
screwing over girls. I don't think you can ever choose
who you're attracted to. If you had asked me what my
type was the day before I met Jason, I would have described his opposite—I would have described someone
like Stephen. But then Jason came onto the scene, and
it was all over. Liking Jason wasn't anything I could
choose, or anything I could control." Remember *Gone*

with the Wind? Scarlet O'Hara didn't *want* to love Rhett Butler—in fact, she couldn't even stand him. But sometimes there's no controlling your heart.

"In the end, you're going to love who you love," Lauren says, "and there's nothing anyone can say to change that—even you. But if you fall for a Bad Boy, be ready for everything that comes with it, and remember: people hardly ever change. Have fun, but don't expect to turn his life around. And if it ever stops being fun, get out while the good times and fun still outweigh the tears."

WHITNEY'S WISDOM ON BAD BOYS

"Every girl wants one thing," says Whitney. "Every girl wants what they can't have." Truer words were never spoken.

Whitney says Bad Boys appeal to a woman's competitive side—and what girl doesn't like a good challenge? "Girls like Bad Boys because they represent a

challenge. If you know you can have a guy within the first five minutes of meeting him, you're going to be interested for about five minutes. But Bad Boys are hard to pin down, and that's a big part of their attraction. When a guy makes himself unavailable, that just makes girls want him that much more." Of course, the opposite is true also. Bad Girls are a topic for another book, but even all of us good girls know that guys always want you more when they can't have you.

One of the girls' friends was dating a new guy who was iffy about the whole situation. He wasn't sure he wanted a girlfriend right now, maybe yes, maybe no, blah blah. Then her ex-boyfriend came to visit. All of a sudden, the new guy was writing her passionate e-mails at 3 a.m. and running a marathon to prove how much manlier he was than the ex-boyfriend. It just took that hint of unavailability to push him over the edge.

Of course, at the end of the day, no self-respecting girl should want a guy who treats her badly. "But girls do want a guy who keeps them guessing," Whitney says, "Predictability is boring. It's the mystery that makes a relationship exciting."

Although Whitney doesn't necessarily fall for classic Bad Boys, she understands the appeal of a guy who keeps a girl on her toes: "Every girl is attracted to a guy who understands a woman's mind. Those are the guys who know when to call and when not to call, when to back off a little, and when to come on strong. It's all about their timing. Bad Boys just seem to know how to run those little games, and that keeps things interesting." Of course interesting is great for a while, but if you're looking for something more—say, a stable, mature, fulfilling relationship—you'd better start looking somewhere else.

"Bad Boys do get a lot of attention from girls," Whitney says, "but I really don't think it's the 'bad' that women are attracted to. Bad Boys just have better instincts, they're unpredictable, and you're always wondering what they're going to do next." So it's really not that all girls love Bad Boys—it's just that no girls love boring guys.

HOW HEIDI HANDLES HER BAD BOY

Heidi's got her own personal Bad Boy: Spencer. He's devilish, exciting, and experienced at getting what he wants, when he wants it. But according to Heidi, all of

Spencer's Bad Boy traits just make him that much more appealing: "If you can take a wild guy who's known for breaking hearts and make him your boyfriend, that's great. If you can make that guy fall in love, that's the ultimate. I'm a competitive girl, and I love a good challenge. There's no bigger challenge than a Bad Boy."

"Spencer has been called a Bad Boy. He's been called a villain, and he's been called worse. But I know I love Spencer, and I know he's the sweetest man in the world. There's no denying that Spencer does what it takes to get what he wants. That might cause people to call him a Bad Boy, but I just call him honest. We're all trying to get what we want—Spencer just doesn't apologize for it."

Heidi says that she's learned a lot from Spencer and his Bad Boy ways: "Ever since I met him, Spencer has set huge goals for himself and he's accomplished every single one of them. People who get things done don't get that way by worrying about what strangers think of them. Personally, I think more people should worry about going for what they want and worry less about me and Spencer."

"Everyone asks me how I can be in love with a Bad Boy. I always ask, 'What exactly has he done that's so bad?' Is it the charity work he's so involved in? Is it all the support he's given me, and all the effort he's put into our relationship?"

"I've learned more from Spencer than I have from anyone else in my life. He taught me what kind of woman I want to be. I realized I was so flirty before I started going out with him. Spencer is an extremely savvy businessman, and he's taught me to recognize when I'm being played. I see now that I was played not only in business, but also by my friends. He's taught me to stand up for myself, and how to fight for what I deserve."

"Spencer taught me that sometimes the people you have to watch out for most are your girlfriends. Sometimes your girlfriends say they're your true friends, but they won't really be there for you. Sometimes, your girlfriends act out of jealousy, not friendship."

"The most important thing Spencer has taught me is to appreciate the moment. We always make the most of the precious time we have here and never waste a moment worrying what anybody thinks. So if that's being a Bad Boy, then, yes, I guess I love Bad Boys."

Let Them Own Their Own Mistakes

· ·

He left the toilet seat up—again—and you almost took a bath last time you sat down. He still owes you an apology for canceling on that dinner with your parents. And you'd think he'd manage to wipe off the coffee table after his boozy buddies were over for the football-and-nacho-cheese-dip bonanza two days ago.

You may not be able to control a guy's behavior, but you can control your own. Sometimes, you might have to let things slide—the toilet seat, for instance. Others, the guys need to own, no matter how much they hate it—dinner with your parents. Here are Lauren's rules for dealing with a lifetime of annoying boy mistakes.

HOW LAUREN HOLDS BOYS TO THEIR OWN MISTAKES

"Boys make their own mistakes, so let them make their own excuses," advises Lauren. "I never make excuses for boys."

Unfortunately, Lauren has spent a lot of time helping a lot of crying friends: "While I'm telling them soothing things, stroking their hair, and wiping their runny noses, I have two goals: one, to make my friend feel better, and two, to make the boys who did this to them suffer." Think of Charlotte in the *Sex and the City* movie telling Big that she cursed the day he was born. Funny, of course, especially since she was going into labor at the time, but also true—girlfriends always need to defend each other against hurt inflicted by boys.

"But the funny thing is that a lot of the time girls aren't furious with the boys who put them in this situation. They actually make *excuses* for them. They come up with reasons why it's not the guy's fault. Girls try to make themselves feel better by denying the fact that she's dating losers. No one wants to believe that the guy they're dating just doesn't care that much about her or her feelings." Girls also worry that there's something wrong with *them* for choosing a guy who would hurt them so badly.

Everyone makes mistakes, and Lauren believes that people should own up to their flaws: "Boyfriends are supposed to make your life happy, not sad. They're supposed to make you feel good, not bad. Whether or not he meant to do it, if you're crying into your friend's shoulder, your boyfriend messed up. There's no need to make excuses for him."

"When you give a guy a free pass once, it's just the beginning of a long series of heartbreaks," Lauren says. "Guaranteed, he'll let you down a hundred more times, and why wouldn't he? He knows that you will not only forgive him, but you'll even make up his excuses for him!" Lauren's not big on excuses, but even she's made mistakes. When Jason showed up in her life again, she was all set to take him back. She just needed a little bit of encouragement. Then he pulled another Jason-worthy move: he sprang it on her that he had a new girlfriend. Not a word about this chick before, of course. Lauren did a good job of not falling apart, but she was completely thrown off-balance.

It's not that Lauren doesn't believe in forgiveness: "I'm all about second chances. I've made screwups in every relationship I've ever been in, so I'm glad I was given a chance to redeem myself. But I always took responsibility and admitted when I screwed up. Boys should be man enough to do the same thing. Let them own up to their own mistakes. Don't let them feed you excuses and, whatever you do, never make excuses for them."

Whitney's "Five Things Every Guy Can Get Right"

1. **Keep It Casual**

   "Don't choose a stuffy restaurant or a formal environment for the first date. You can get fancier on later dates, but start off by choosing some place nice and laid-back."

   Think blue jeans, not ball gowns.

2. **Be Prompt**

   "This is the very first impression the girl will get, so make it a good one. Showing up on time shows you're thoughtful, responsible, and can plan ahead. Showing up late means you start the date by apologizing."

   Set an alarm, write yourself a note, or do whatever it takes to get you to her doorstep on time. Punctuality is an important quality in a man, and one of the easiest qualities to demonstrate.

3. **Stay Active and Stay Fed**

   "Go someplace where you can get up and actually *do* something. Bowling and miniature golf are good because they provide a little competition, and something to laugh about. It takes some of the pressure off the conversation."

Wherever you go, make sure there's food there, and make sure there's a menu where everyone can find something they'll eat. (Don't bring a vegetarian to a steak house!) You don't want to ruin a perfectly good evening by sending your date home hungry.

4. **Listen!**

"You can talk about almost anything you want. Just make sure you occasionally talk about something other than yourself."

Ask questions. Find out what your date likes. Be interested.

And if you can't be interested, at least *sound* interested!

5. **Take a Chance**

"If the date was smooth, you've both had fun, and you're feeling confident, you may decide to go in for a kiss. If you feel like it's the thing to do, there's no reason not to give it a try. No one can make this judgment for you. You just have to read the situation."

If the rest of the date went well and you're a gentleman about it, going for the kiss isn't taking too huge of a risk. Even if the girl says no, sometimes it's still nice for her to know you are interested.

Dealing with Jealous Boyfriends

• •

All boys get jealous at some point—and girls do too. Usually, a little "Why aren't you talking to me?" jealousy is nothing to worry about. As long as no one's feelings are being hurt, it just means that your boy wants you to pay attention to him more than other guys—perfect!

Of course, there's a difference between wanting you to stand next to him at a party and standing guard outside the door to your apartment all night. You want a boyfriend, not your own personal stalker.

Here's one strategy for controlling jealousy before it becomes a major problem.

HOW TO HANDLE JEALOUSY LIKE A HEIDI

When boyfriends get jealous, Heidi starts pointing fingers—at their girlfriends.

"All men get jealous, and it's part of your job as a girlfriend to make your man comfortable. If he's jealous, you're doing a bad job. It's not that difficult."

Heidi believes that giving her guy undivided attention is the least she can do. After all, that's what she expects in return: "I know that being my boyfriend is a big job. I need a lot of attention, and I want to be treated like a princess. The man who's prince enough to do that deserves to know that I'm with him and *only* him, one hundred percent of the time." If it makes your guy happy, hold his hand in public. Kiss him in front of other people (be careful on that one—some guys love PDA, some avoid it like the plague). Tell him in your most sincere way that he's the only guy for you—then do him the courtesy of not checking out other guys when you're together in public.

So why do so many men spend so much time being jealous of so many women? "Girls are crazy," Heidi says. "I see girls all the time who go to a club and completely ignore their boyfriends. They're out there laughing, flirting, and hanging on random guys while their boyfriends are getting angry on the other side of the room. Then when their boyfriend gets upset, they say, 'I just don't know why he gets so jealous.' I'm like, 'Really? Are you that dense?'"

Sometimes, your guy might be overreacting, of course. Examples: talking to another guy briefly at the bar while getting a drink: okay. Talking to another guy at the bar for half an hour while your guy waits back at the table: not okay. Giving a guy friend a hug: okay. Giving a guy friend a nice peck on the lips: not okay.

Sitting beside a guy while chatting: okay. Sitting on his lap: not okay.

Heidi says that girls should examine their behavior: "Your boyfriend is acting jealous because *you're* making him feel insecure. That's why the worst thing you can do is argue. If he's already unsure, frustrated, and humiliated, when you go looking for a fight, you will find one one hundred percent of the time, and it won't be pretty. Instead, ask yourself why he's feeling jealous. Whether or not you've actually given him something to be jealous about doesn't really matter. You're supposed to be on his team, and you're supposed to make him feel good. You obviously weren't doing that, so it's no one's fault but your own."

HOW AUDRINA AVOIDS JEALOUS BOYS

Audrina would rather just avoid the jealousy game altogether. "A little jealousy means the guy cares," she says. "Too much jealousy means 'Bye-bye.'"

"Justin and I used to play the Jealousy Game," Audrina remembers. "He'd see me talking to a guy, and he'd get all mad. At the time, it seemed like a good way to get his attention . . . until I'd turn around and see him talking to another girl. Then I'd be the one who got mad. That's why the Jealousy Game never works. It never brings you closer together, and it always makes you fight." This kind of game does not signal a good relationship. If you're both secure in caring for each other, you won't need to compete like this. Your guy should *want* to pay attention to you because, after all, isn't his girlfriend (that would be you) the cutest, funniest, most attractive girl in the room?

Audrina thinks being overly jealous is a huge turn-off: "When I was dating Bernard, I saw a side of him that I really didn't like. We were out in Big Bear, and some guys came up to me and said hi. They were just being nice, but Bernard let me know he didn't appreciate it."

That's when Audrina knew things were never going to work out between them: "There's something sweet about a guy who shows interest and wants you all to himself, but there's nothing attractive about a guy who's crazy jealous."

Now, Audrina tries to avoid jealousy before it becomes an issue. "If Justin and I are at a party, and I'm away from him for a while, I'll smile at him from across the room, just to remind him I'm there with him. And if he's talking to someone else, he'll make eye contact with me, just to stay connected. We still totally do our own thing. We just let each other know that no matter where we are or who we're talking to, at the end of the night, we're going to end up together."

Too Much Too Fast

Most of us have the same dream about falling in love. After that fateful first date, he'll call to tell you he's counting the minutes until he can see you again. Then the flowers start, a different bouquet every day. Then the nightly phone calls—even if you just saw him that afternoon. And the text messages popping up at random times: "Just thinking of you!" "Do you like teddy bears?" "This rose isn't as gorgeous as you are." He wants you to meet his parents—and his brother, and his friends, and his grandmother, and his entire high school class. In fact, what he'd really like to do is surgically attach you to his arm.

This is what we all want, right? Well, maybe not. A guy who comes on too strong can be as infuriating as a guy who won't commit.

After Justin's chilly distance, Audrina thought it was nice that her new guy, Bernard, was attentive and so eager to be with her. She quickly learned that when you fast-forward a relationship, you sometimes reach the end sooner.

HOW AUDRINA SCRAPED OFF "BERNARD THE BARNACLE"

"A good relationship is one where you spend a lot of time with the other person," Audrina says, "but you still have enough time for yourself."

Audrina recently dated a guy named Bernard. She had grown up with him in Orange County, so they immediately felt comfortable with each other, and they were able to skip a few of the initial getting-to-know-you stages. Unfortunately, Bernard wanted to jump from that all the way to BF/GF.

Audrina remembers how much Bernard liked to spend time with her: "He'd come up for dinner and end up staying the night. He'd come up for the night and end up staying the weekend. I'd try to give him a hint that it was time for him to leave, but he just never picked up on it. It was like he was stuck to me, and I couldn't shake him. Lauren started calling him Bernard the Barnacle."

Bernard invited Audrina to Lake Tahoe that winter: "It was a little early in the relationship to make a trip together, but it was only for a weekend, so I decided to go anyway. Unfortunately, an unexpected blizzard rolled through, and we were snowed in for almost a week. I didn't know anyone else in Tahoe, it was just all Bernard, all the time. I would have thought he'd grow sick of me in that time, but he seemed perfectly comfortable spending twenty-four hours a day together."

"I really like to have my own space and my own time, but Bernard kept making plans for the two of us. My sister had just had a baby, and I really wanted to be around for that. He couldn't understand that I couldn't be with him all the time. When I told him I needed alone time, he thought I was blowing him off."

Audrina did like spending time with Bernard, and all the attention and consistency was a nice change from Justin Bobby. But when Bernard rushed to put labels on them, Audrina knew things had gone too far: "He started throwing around words like 'relationship' and calling me his 'girlfriend.' It got to the point where he'd make travel plans for us, and he wouldn't even ask me. That's when I realized that this wasn't something I wanted. I wanted to date Bernard and get to know him. I didn't want to jump into a crazy, serious relationship like I was married all of a sudden. I finally had to sit Bernard down and tell him I wasn't ready to be in a serious relationship."

So if you're wishing for a guy to come sweep you off your feet, be careful what you wish for. It's nice when an interested guy comes along, but once in a while it's nice for him to go.

9

TRICKS OF
THE TRADE

Flip the Script

● ●

You make sure you're sexy, fresh, and funny. You flirt a little, but not too much. You joke and laugh. You go out with groups, on single dates, on double dates. But no matter what you do, you're still not getting what you want from guys, even though you're trying lots of different types. Well, short of entering a convent, something's going to have to change. And that something . . . is you.

If you feel as if you're always the one waiting, doubting, and second-guessing, it may be time to rewrite your game plan. Take a different approach, and let someone else do the worrying for a while.

HOW TO TAKE THE LEAD LIKE A LAUREN

After trying every dating strategy she could think of to no avail, Lauren decided to take a different approach: date like a guy. Does that mean wearing the same polo shirt three nights in a row and always showing up ten minutes late?

No—it just means taking the lead for a while. "In most relationships," Lauren explains, "it's always the girls who get hurt, and the girls who end up crying. I don't want to be that girl anymore. I want to turn the tables."

"Whenever I can, I'm the pursuer, not the pursued. I'm not afraid to go up to a guy in a club and tell him to come sit with my friends and me. Sometimes, I'll use a line. I'll look at him like I recognize him and say, 'Where do I know you from?' Other times, when

I'm feeling really brave, I'll just walk up to a cute guy and start talking." To tell the truth, most guys would probably be flattered that you noticed them. He might even be relieved that now he doesn't have the pressure of trying to start a conversation with *you*.

"My friends tell me that they think of me as a relationship girl, but I go through times that I don't want a boyfriend at all. And sometimes when I do want a boyfriend, I want a fun boyfriend, rather than a good one—and that's a very big difference. The boy who makes the best choice isn't necessarily the boy who'll be the most fun."

"Dating like a guy means you have the freedom to

make those mistakes. You can have crushes that you know won't last. You can date a guy who will like you for a while and then go away. And you can do it all on your own terms, so you know you won't get hurt." One of the biggest differences between guys and girls is that guys tend not to think about things the way girls do. This doesn't mean their brains are empty—it just means that they're not much for analysis. They just *do*, without thinking, "Should I? But what if? Or I could . . ." Sometimes it works, sometimes it doesn't, but either way, guys aren't going to get too worked up. It's nothing personal, they might figure, if a girl rejects them for a date. Or, too bad, she's cute. Oh, well. On to the next one.

Of course, you may not always want to do everything a guy would do. Lauren says, "You can't *always* date like a boy. After all, no guy has a rule about not kissing on the first date like I do. Most guys don't have a policy about not returning the first phone call. You end up taking pages out of both playbooks. You take the lead like a guy when you don't feel like waiting around, and when you start to get what you want, you pull back a little."

"Dating is supposed to be fun. If guys keep breaking your heart and making you cry, then you must be doing something wrong. You need to flip the script once in a while and take back control. You need to try dating like a guy."

HOW HEIDI HAS CHANGED HER HABITS

Not everyone subscribes to Lauren's "date like a guy" method. In true guy fashion, Heidi asked out Spencer, not the other way around—and to this day she regrets it.

"Obviously, I'm absolutely thrilled to be going out with Spencer," she says, "but the first time we went out, I made all the wrong moves. Instead of holding back from him and building the mystery, I laid out all my emotions and went for it. I would change that if I could."

"We were at a club and we were having a great time. We were laughing, we were having great conversation, and really connecting. I was thinking to myself, 'I finally found a guy who can keep up with me.' But for some reason, Spencer didn't ask me out. I decided to go for it."

"I was pretty casual about it. I just sort of floated a

'Let's hang out,' and he took me up on it. It may seem like, 'Great. It worked perfectly. What's the problem?' It was the biggest mistake I could have made."

"When you remain a little cool and distant," Heidi says, "men think of you as desirable and mysterious. When you make yourself open and available, men tend to think of you as open and available. No guy gives his best for something he thinks he can always easily have. Predictably, Spencer and I fizzled the first time around, but I learned from my mistake." There's nothing wrong with maintaining a little mystery, as Heidi suggests. But you do want to make sure that eventually you're just being yourself around your guy—no games, no pretending. That's the only way you'll be able to go the distance.

A few months later, Heidi and Spencer reconnected. This time, Heidi knew just what to do to have Spencer eating from the palm of her hand: "When we started hanging out a second time, I turned the tables. I wasn't going to be as available, I wasn't going to be so obvious about my interest, and I definitely wasn't going to be asking him out anymore."

"I put the pressure on him to come after me. He'd have to make the first moves, he'd have to do the asking out, and he was going to have to chase me a little bit. He's been chasing me ever since!"

Audrina's Good Date/Bad Date

Good Date:

"He talks interestingly about things you both enjoy."

Bad Date:

"He talks about his old girlfriends. That's the rudest thing a guy can do. Nothing is a bigger turnoff."

Good Date:

"He's respectful. He waits for you to begin eating and behaves like a gentleman."

Bad Date:

"He burps. Even Justin couldn't get away with this. He used to burp all the time, and I couldn't stand it."

Good Date:

"He keeps steady eye contact with you."

Bad Date:

"He checks out other girls, flirts with the waitress. He picks up his phone."

Good Date:

"He's clean, showered, dressed up, and he smells good."

Bad Date:

"He hasn't showered in two weeks, and he picked his outfit from the bottom of the hamper."

● ● ●

Beauty Never Breaks

You spent an hour trying on everything in your closet. You've loofahed, exfoliated, deep-conditioned, flat-ironed, blow-dried, spritzed, sprayed, ironed, static-guarded, and de-linted. The hair is perfectly tousled, the dress is sleek and silky, the heels are Manolos, the fragrance is Jo Malone. When the doorbell rings, there's no doubt about it. You look good.

But aside from a few dashes to the ladies' room, all

that primping and prepping stops once you walk out your front door. What was tousled at seven is just messy by ten. By the time you two hit the club, the sleek dress is creased, the Manolos are giving you a blister, and all that Jo Malone is buried under the garlic fumes emanating from your every pore (how were you supposed to know what was in the shrimp scampi? It's not called shrimp garlic). Much as you hate to admit it, you're no longer the radiant maiden you were at the beginning of the night.

No fear! You don't have to end the evening like a train wreck. Whitney offers a few ingenious tricks that will keep you looking and feeling fresh all night long.

HOW TO STAY FRESH AS A WHITNEY

First, bring back the Jo Malone. "I always have nice perfume," says Whitney. "Not only do I put it on before I go out, but I bring the bottle with me. Obviously, if you're at a crowded concert or a hot bar, you're going to want to dab on a little more, but I think it's always a good idea to reapply. Guys are amazingly responsive to smell, even more than they're probably aware of. Guys

will be a lot more responsive to you when you always smell good." Remember, don't apply perfume in public or do any grooming at all, including hair combing. The only thing you can do is apply a little lip gloss with the tip of your finger. You can also dab your nose with powder from a compact. Otherwise, do it in the restroom. There's nothing nastier than watching someone brush her hair at the dinner table.

Then, vanquish the garlic. "I always carry a pack of gum," Whitney reveals. After all, it doesn't do much good to smell like flowers if your breath smells like garlic. "It seems like a small thing, but when dinner includes onions and coffee, not having a pack of gum can become a very big thing. I know that bad breath is a gigantic turnoff for me, so the thought that my breath is bad makes me really insecure. I keep a pack on me at all times, so I can order whatever I want and never have to worry." There's nothing wrong with whipping out the gum after a meal and offering your guy a piece. Just make sure it's a mint flavor. You don't want to be offering around the Bubblicious grape on a date—not if you want him to think you're older than ten.

"Three, knives make perfect mirrors. You can only go to the bathroom to check yourself in the mirror so many times, but your knife is in front of you all throughout dinner. The only thing worse than having bad breath is having a disgusting piece of chewed food caught between your teeth. Whenever I have a second to myself, I hold the knife horizontally and check my smile for scraps. It's saved me some embarrassment on a couple of occasions!" If you do find you have (horror!) a piece of spinach between your teeth, try to avoid picking it out right there. No one wants to watch that little operation. Go to the restroom. If you absolutely can't excuse yourself right then, try to scrape at it discreetly with the tip of your little finger. Keep your lips closed and he might not even notice.

"Everyone has their own little tricks," says Whitney, "but these work the best for me. Just knowing that

I smell good, my breath is fresh, and I don't have dinner stuck in my teeth is enough to make me feel confident. The best thing is that I'm able to check these things anywhere I go."

Secrets of a Serial Dater

* * * * * * * * * * * * * * * * * * *

The girls have all done more than their fair share of dating, but of the four, no one's logged more hours than Audrina. She didn't get the title serial dater *for nothing.*

Audrina has picked up quite a bit of wisdom over her dating life. Some of these tips she's learned by seeing what works well. Others she's learned by seeing what does not work at all.

Here are three of Audrina's most valuable insider tips to help you on your way.

TIP #1: DEVISE AN ESCAPE PLAN "At the beginning of every date, let the guy know that there's someplace else you *might* have to go," Audrina says, "even if there isn't."

The first reason for setting up an imaginary Plan B is obvious: "If it ends up being a boring date, you can just say, 'Uh-oh, my friend is calling. It turns out I do need to go meet her after all. Bye-bye!' It won't sound like an excuse because you warned him before the night even started."

The other reason is pure genius: "When a guy thinks he might only have a little bit of time with you, he enjoys it more. He makes the most of every minute because you might have to take off all of a sudden. He's going to have a better time because you're making your time seem more valuable."

TIP #2: HAVE A SIGNATURE SCENT Audrina's next tip takes advantage of men's strong reliance on the sense of smell. "If you want to make a lasting impression on a guy," Audrina advises, "wear the same perfume every time you see him."

"Smell brings back the strongest memories, so whenever he smells that perfume—even if it's on someone else—he'll think of you. I've had guys call me and say, 'I just smelled your scent and it made me think of you.' It's pretty nice to be able to make a guy think about you when you're not even around."

"You don't have to wear the same perfume every day. One guy can be Marc Jacobs, another guy can be Jo Malone."

TIP #3: LIMIT WHAT YOU DRINK "It's obvious, but it's important," says Audrina. "Drinking a lot of alcohol on a date is always a mistake."

How to Read a Man's Shoes like a Lauren

• • • • • • •

"Shoes tell you how much care a guy puts into his appearance, how much thought he put into the date, and they say a lot about the guy's personal taste." Here's what Lauren makes of a few different pairs.

If the Guy Wears Flip-Flops . . .

"It says he didn't make an effort. Flip-flops are perfect for the beach or a casual barbecue, but if you're taking a girl out in Hollywood, you need to step it up a little."

"Brody not only wore flip-flops on a date," Lauren recalls, "but he wore flip-flops with, like, a suit. Enough said."

If the Guy Wears Nice Leather Shoes . . .

"It means he probably has a good job. He takes pride in his appearance, and he thinks enough of you to get dressed up for you."

"Men's dress shoes aren't the most comfortable thing in the world," Lauren says. "Of course, they're nowhere near as torturous as girls' shoes, but the fact that the guy put on something *slightly* uncomfortable means that he's willing to go out of his way for you."

If the Guy Wears Great Sneakers . . .

"It means he has great taste, but they have to be the *right* sneakers."

"Unless they're really stylish and very hip, then they're just sneakers," Lauren says. "It's impressive when a guy can pick out the perfect pair."

If the Guy Wears Boots . . .

"He's probably a little too rock-and-roll for me."

"Justin Bobby once wore combat boots to a beach barbecue. I guess that's making a fashion statement, but I just feel like there's no need for boots in Southern California."

If the Guy's Shoes Are Pointier than Yours . . .

"Run!"

● ● ●

This is one of those lessons that Audrina learned the hard way: "I was out with a guy named Chris, a co-worker from Epic Records. He lives in Venice, and we were getting some drinks at a sushi restaurant called Chaya. They serve these really sweet-tasting shots that don't taste like they'd be strong. I usually try to watch what I drink, especially on a first date, but I'd never had these before and I thought I'd be okay. I guess I was wrong."

"Half an hour later I was getting sick in the bathroom, while my date was talking to me on the other side of the door, bringing me glasses of water. It doesn't matter who you are—it's hard to vomit and be sexy at the same time. Chris was really nice about it, but our first date was also our last."

Audrina doesn't think anything is worth the risk of overdoing it on a date: "It's always better to have too little than too much. So if you're wondering whether or not you should have another drink, the answer is always no."

10

THE END OF
THE ROAD

Dropping the Hammer

* *

Conversation on dates has deteriorated to one-word an-swers and mumbling. You answer the door in sweatpants and don't care that it's him. The other day, you found yourselves having a screaming match over where to go for frozen yogurt. You're just not feeling it anymore—the time has come for the relationship to end. But since you're the one who's decided to end it, that means you're going to have to tackle the most unpleasant task in dating: the breakup.

If you have a soul and a beating heart, you don't enjoy breaking up with people. And the longer you've been with the person, the harder it is. But sooner or later, we all have to dump someone, as sure as, sooner or later, we all get dumped.

If starting a relationship is tricky, then ending one requires practically UN-level diplomatic skills. Of course, you can always move, fake your own death, or join the Witness Protection Program. Or, you can try the honest approach.

Here's some advice on how to tackle the challenge of the breakup head-on. You can expect it to hurt a little bit, but there's something to be said for getting it over with quickly.

HOW WHITNEY HITS THE BRAKES

"When it's time to end a relationship, I don't like to prolong the pain," Whitney says. "I like to rip off the Band-Aid."

Whitney believes that when you dump a guy, you

have to do your own dirty work, and you have to be brave about it: "There is one and only one way to break up with a boy: in person, face-to-face, and one hundred percent honest."

"Don't freeze him out or gradually stop returning his phone calls. That's lame, and how would you feel if someone you liked and trusted did that to you? Don't prolong it by waiting for the perfect time. There is no perfect time, and all you're doing by putting it off is wasting his time and yours—he's never going to thank you for that."

"Don't sugarcoat it or make it sound like you're going through a temporary thing that you might get over. Show him the respect he deserves. Sit him down and let him know in no uncertain terms: this is not going to work out." Even if you're mad at him, try to avoid accusations. Don't dredge up old arguments to make the point about why you should break up. It's going to hurt enough that you're doing it, without reminding him of all the ways he's screwed up in the past. Be honest. Be kind. Be brief. Later, he'll thank you for all of these—especially the kind and brief parts.

Whitney wasn't always so honest with guys when their time was up: "In the past, I've tried to dodge having to break up by letting us drift apart or blowing a guy off. But in the end, I always feel bad, and I end up calling the guy. I let him know that I'm no longer interested, and if he wants to know, I'll even tell him why." Face-to-face is best, phone is a distant second. But no matter what, *do not* break up with someone on e-mail, text, or IM. Or voice mail. Even if he's the biggest slime in the universe, he deserves ten minutes over coffee.

"There's *always* a reason, and the guy deserves to know. Even if I'm just too busy to have a boyfriend, I have no problem telling him that. I'm honest about my reasons, but I've found it's possible to be honest without hurting their feelings. You're just trying to end the relationship, not scar the guy for life." There's nothing wrong with resorting to a few stock phrases. "I don't think we have a future together" is a good one, as is "This isn't working out for me."

Telling a guy you want to stop seeing him romantically is always a tough conversation. But if you have the courage and the honesty to do it right, it's a conversation that you have to have only once. As Whitney says, "Do him a favor and do *yourself* a favor: say what you mean so you can both move on with your lives."

HOW TO END IT LIKE
AN AUDRINA

"If I care about a guy and he's been nice and sweet," says Audrina, "I'll break up face-to-face."

According to Audrina, sitting down with the guy is the only decent thing to do, although it does have its dangers: "Breaking up with someone in person is the most respectful way to break up with someone, but it's

also the trickiest. When a guy gets really sad or flashes you those puppy-dog eyes, it can be difficult to go through with."

"In high school, I knew I wanted to break up with my boyfriend Richie, but every time I started, I felt too bad and would lose my nerve. The relationship dragged on for another couple of months!"

Now whenever Audrina is going into battle, she has a game plan. "I'm not good at just spontaneously dumping someone, so I try to prepare. First, I plan out what I'm going to say, and then I actually write it down. Then, I think of all the comebacks that he may say."

Finally, Audrina does some role-playing . . . with her mother. "Before I break up with any boyfriend, I break up with my mother. She plays the role of the guy, and I give her my little speech. I'll tell my mom, 'This isn't working out. It's not you, it's me. I think we should start seeing other people.' Then my mom does what the guy would do and tries to talk me out of it. I practice all my comebacks until I'm ready for any scenario. After breaking up with your mom, breaking up with a guy is easy."

Reverse Psychology

· ·

Breaking up with someone is a messy business. You have to look a person that you care about in the eye and tell him you don't like him as much as he likes you. If you're too honest, you could really hurt his feelings. If you're too gentle, he may just not get the point.

Lauren has come up with a strategy where she never has to break up with anyone. With her method, she's able to avoid all drawn-out relationship talks and difficult breakups. Never again will she have to say, "It's not you, it's me."

HOW LAUREN LETS THE BREAKUP COME TO HER

"I would rather get dumped than break up with someone," Lauren says. "So instead of breaking up with people, I try to get dumped."

This may seem like a strange strategy, but Lauren

will do almost anything to avoid having a painful, emotional breakup with a guy who likes her more than she likes him: "First, I avoid seeing them. Then, I stop returning their calls. I just become a generally frustrating person. I piss them off until they don't want to deal with me anymore. Then they have to dump me."

Lauren finds getting dumped a lot easier than

Whitney's Good Date/Bad Date

Good Date:
"There's an equal amount of talking on both sides of the table. Not only does he ask you questions, but he actually *listens* to your answers."

Bad Date:
"He's the only one talking, and the only thing he's talking about is himself. No matter what you do to change the subject, it's 'One, two, three—back to me!'"

Good Date:
"Good manners show a sense of pride, and his manners are impeccable. He keeps his napkin on his lap and his elbows off the table. He could come to dinner at the Port household—where manners are strictly enforced—and the whole family would be impressed with his etiquette."

Bad Date:

"He chews with his mouth open, smacks his lips, and shows you his food with every bite. Your gag reflex is triggered every time he slurps his soup. You're praying he doesn't order dessert."

Good Date:

"He calls the next day to let you know he had a nice time."

Bad Date:

"He waits a week, then texts you at midnight: 'S'up? U partying?'"

• • •

breaking up—especially when she brought it on herself. No nervous speeches, no drama, no boy tears. She lets the guy speak his mind and save face, but in the end she gets what she wants: to be single and free of the guy.

Sometimes the guy doesn't even have a chance to do the breaking up because Lauren won't answer any of his calls. "I'm pretty sure there are a few people that I never actually broke up with. It's been a few years now, but it never came to an official end. Now that I think of it, I have several boyfriends!"

Hold Your Friend Up as She Lets Him Down

We've all been there—your phone rings. You answer, but you can't talk to your friend because she's sobbing so hard. You put down the remote and grab the car keys in anticipation of a night of crying, massive doses of ice cream, and reassurances that he was a jerk anyway. That's what you do when your friend gets dumped. But when she's doing the dumping, the situation is a little more delicate.

Being a good friend is about saying all the things a person needs to hear while still staying in touch with reality. It's not enough to shower someone with praise and pretend that nothing's wrong. You have to deal truthfully with the facts, painful as they may be, but reassure your friend that no matter how hard this is, she will get through it.

When Audrina caught Justin with another girl, she decided she couldn't put up with his behavior any longer. She knew she had to break up with him, and she knew it was going to be painful. Audrina was in need of a friend while she let Justin down. Luckily, she had Lauren.

HOW TO BE THERE THROUGH THE BREAKUP LIKE A LAUREN

"Breaking up with a guy can be as upsetting as getting dumped," says Lauren. "I know what it's like to feel pain over breaking up with someone, so I try to be there for my friends who are going through that."

"I was the one who broke up with Jason, but it was still one of the hardest periods of my life," Lauren says. "If he had broken up with me, I'm sure all my friends would have called, visited, and sent flowers. I think when you're the one who initiates the breakup, people mistakenly assume you're okay."

Lauren made sure she was there for Audrina the night Audrina broke up with Justin: "She was playing it over and over again in her head, questioning whether she made the right decision. I just told her how proud I was of her, and that I knew she had done the right thing."

"Some guys just have mind control over you," Lauren says. "When you have a good reason to get mad at them, they find a way of making you feel crazy or silly. Justin took mind control to a new level—he had Audrina questioning what she had seen with her own eyes."

"We had all seen Justin kissing another girl at a bar, but he almost made her believe that she imagined it. She needed someone to tell her that she wasn't crazy, and that he had done hurtful, disrespectful things. I let her know that she's this beautiful girl, inside and out, and she didn't have to put up with that. I just kept reminding her that she had finally gotten closure on a long, painful situation. The hardest part was over."

Now, Audrina just needed something to take her mind off Justin. "Audrina had been really strong and didn't give Justin any tears," Lauren says, "but Audrina looked like she still had a good cry in her. I told her to

Top Breakup Songs

Lauren

Sinéad O'Connor, "Nothing Compares 2 U"

Whitney

The Kooks, "Do You Love Me Still?"

Audrina

OneRepublic, "Apologize"

A Fine Frenzy, "Almost Lover"

Heidi

Leona Lewis, "Bleeding Love"

let it out. I offered to stay in and watch a sad movie, so she could pretend she was crying over that."

But what Audrina really wanted to do was to go out and dance. Lauren was exhausted from a long week of work and school, but she rallied for her friend: "I called some people, took down a bunch of Red Bulls, and we were off to Les Deux. Pretty soon, we were out, we were dancing, we were with our friends, and Justin Bobby was the last thing on Audrina's mind."

He's Found Someone New

· ·

You're cool with your ex. You're way past the voodoo-doll-and-curse stage. You don't feel the need to cross to the other side of the street when you see him. In fact, the two of you are so completely cool that you can even do things such as go for coffee together. See how calm and mature you are? You want your ex to be happy, get over you, and start dating again . . . just not before you find someone new first.

Unfortunately, exes don't always cooperate. You've still got that picture of the two of you at the beach on your bulletin board, even if it is hidden under a class schedule, but you've heard that he's already out on the town, filling his cell phone with new numbers.

If seeing your ex is painful, then seeing another girl on the arm of your ex is like having hot needles thrust in your eyes. Here's how to keep your cool when you see your old flame sparking with someone new.

LAUREN'S HOUSEWARMING FROM HELL

"Meeting my ex's new girlfriend wouldn't have been too bad," Lauren says, "if it hadn't been at their engagement party!"

After Lauren broke up with Jason, it didn't take Jason long to start dating someone new. Lauren wasn't surprised. As she puts it, "When a girl gets out of a long relationship, she celebrates her newfound freedom by reconnecting with her girl friends. When a guy gets out of a long relationship, he celebrates his freedom by going out with every girl he can."

So Lauren accepted an invitation to Jason's apartment knowing that it would be a little awkward, but she had no idea what was in store for her: "Audrina and I thought we were going to a housewarming party, and I knew we were going to meet Jason's new girlfriend. We were a little bit dressed up. I was wearing heels and a dress, but when we got there, it was a beer-and-flip-flops-and-keg party. It was a little ridiculous."

"Jason deserves to be with a nice girl," Lauren says, "so I tried really hard to like his girlfriend, but I didn't get the feeling she liked me. She was very quiet around me, and she shot me some funny looks. If

Jason was ever alone with me for two seconds, she'd walk up and start making out with him in front of my face. All in all, everyone was nice, and Audrina and I were doing our best to be supportive of Jason, his new place, and his new relationship."

As much as Lauren was trying to be positive, she couldn't have anticipated what was about to happen next: "Out of the blue, someone raised their glass to make a toast: 'Here's to two of our best friends who just got engaged.' I wondered who they were talking about, until I saw Jason kissing his new girlfriend. I can honestly say that in my whole life I never thought I'd be toasting to that."

"Jason came and found me on the balcony, and he asked me what I thought about his getting married. I could never be fake around Jason, so I told him the truth: I thought he was being dumb for getting married so young. I just think it's going to be hard for him to make a lifetime commitment to someone else when he's still figuring out exactly who *he* wants to be. I definitely don't think marriage is something that should be rushed into. It takes a long time to figure out what kind of person you want to spend the rest of your life with, and you have to kiss a lot of frogs."

The biggest surprise of the evening was not that Jason was getting engaged, but how well Lauren handled the news: "At first, I wasn't sure that I'd be able to deal with Jason dating another girl, so I had no idea how I was going to deal with him being *engaged* to someone else. After all, there were definitely moments when I imagined being married to him. But when I looked around at the people, the surroundings, and at Jason, I realized I was okay with it. I'm happy for Jason if he's happy, but I have higher expectations for myself now. I know how I want my engagement to be, I know how I want my relationship to be, and I'm figuring out who I want my husband to be. When I looked around the room, I knew this wasn't it."

"A part of me will always love Jason, but at that moment I knew I was no longer in love with him. So that night, I didn't get jealous or sad or angry. I felt happy. I felt glad. I felt relief. I just kept telling myself, 'This could've been me. This could've been me.'"

Picking Up the Pieces

There are two kinds of breakups. There is the kind where you stock your freezer with Ben & Jerry's, draw the shades, lock the door, turn off your phone, and cry for a week straight. Then there's the really bad kind.

Breaking up with the guy you met at the club last month is one thing. Breaking up with your BF of two years is another. No doubt you guys have been through a lot together. Now, for whatever reason, the relationship has got to end, but that doesn't mean it's going to be easy. Losing that person will feel like having a hole ripped in your body— but only for a while. You may not believe it at the time, but it does get easier, every day. Think about it: all the people you have ever known have gone through a breakup in every single relationship they've ever been in, until their last relationship. It's that last relationship that should make all the breakups worth it.

So until you find that final guy, you're doomed to suffer a few more painful breakups. Here are our girls' survival tactics for fighting through the darkest moments, and discovering the fastest way back to the happy.

HOW TO HEAL LIKE A WHITNEY

"During the first few days of a breakup, you need a little room to breathe," says Whitney.

"When I broke up with my boyfriend of about two years, I thought it was the hardest thing I've ever had

to go through in my life. Unfortunately, a lot of people knew about it, so a lot of people offered to be around me. They were just trying to be good friends and help out, but I wasn't ready for my friends' help yet. At first, I needed to be alone. I needed to shut out the rest of the world and spend some time by myself to think about the loss." Besides, even though your friends love you, they don't always know exactly what you need. Maybe you're like Audrina and you need to dance the night away at a club. Or maybe you just want to stay in, eat greasy food, and wallow for a while. There's nothing wrong with a little wallowing when you really need it.

Whitney remembers how she dealt with her grief:

"At first, I refused a lot of visits and calls from my friends while I was sorting things out. My friends know me, but I was the only one who went through the relationship, and I was the one who went through the breakup. I needed to figure out how *I* felt before I could hear from anyone else."

Besides friends, family, and large quantities of chocolate, one other thing has been helping people through sad times for thousands of years: music. "I had a supply of 'good cry' records, because sometimes a good cry is the only thing that will make you feel better. A lot of Beatles songs have melodies that could push me over the edge and lyrics that made me weep. And when I was really feeling emotional, I'd listen to an electronic band called Ratatat. Their music doesn't even have words—just the melodies were enough to bring tears." Anything that helps you out is going to be a good thing. Write in your journal—nasty letters to your ex, or otherwise. Gather up the mementos of your relationship and do something symbolic with them. If it means enshrining them in a box forever, do it. Or you might want to burn them, depending on your state of mind.

Whatever you do, you also need to keep the relationship and the breakup in perspective, Whitney reminds us. "Although I did allow myself a grieving period, I always kept in mind that it was going to end at

Audrina's Bad-Date Timeline No. 2

8:45   Bernard picks Audrina up. Immediately, his hair is a problem. The hair on top of his head is scooped to a point. The hair in back is longer and shaggy. It can only be described as a Fauxhawk/mullet.

9:15   Audrina tells Bernard that she'll be working at the Grammys. Bernard asks if the Grammys will be canceled due to the writers' strike.

Audrina reminds Bernard that the Grammys are for music, not movies.

9:25   Bernard orders a quesadilla. Tragically, he pronounces the *l*'s. Audrina repeats his mangled pronunciation back to him to see if he's making a joke.

He's not.

9:40   Bernard tells Audrina that he wants to make a trip from Newport to see her new house, but instead of saying "Newport" he calls it "Newps," and instead of "see" he keeps saying "peep." "I want to come up from Newps and peep it."

Wow.

10:00   Bernard tries to make travel plans with Audrina. Audrina mentions that they've been spending a lot of time together, and maybe it would be good to take a break.

Audrina checks to see if Bernard got the hint.

He didn't.

10:15   Audrina asks Bernard if he'd like to see her sister's baby. "No," he replies, "babies scare me."

This brings on a long, awkward pause.

10:20   The server returns to the table. Bernard observes, "The server has really tiny hands, and he smells like cabbage."

Audrina can do nothing but smile.

10:55   Bernard asks for the check.

In mere minutes, Bernard will be driving Audrina home. She can almost taste it.

11:00   At last, the check comes. "I'm not tired," Bernard says. "Let's go to Goa."

Audrina smiles and braces herself for another two hours with this guy.

• • •

some point. And even through all the tears and the soul-searching, I managed to stay positive. I never lost sight of the fact that I would come out the other side of this experience stronger and better."

Of course, no one can or should feel sorry for herself forever: "After the initial shock, you do want to let your best friends and family back in. It's so important to know that you have great people in your life who will go to great lengths for your happiness. But the first part of getting over any serious relationship is coming to terms with the situation all on your own."

Escaping Your Ex

We've all gone through it. You've thought about it and thought about it, and you're certain that this relationship is bad news. It's more than unhealthy—this relationship is radioactive. You let him know in no uncertain terms that you don't want to see him anymore, not now, not ever. Then, a funny thing happens.

A few weeks go by, and suddenly he doesn't seem that bad. With a little distance, you start remembering his most annoying habits as nothing more than funny quirks. You remember his irrational temper as passion. His habit of flirting with other girls is just him being charming. And all the times he behaved badly and hurt your feelings? Maybe you were just being oversensitive. You're lonely. You miss him. You figure it wouldn't hurt to give him a little call and say hello. . . .

A phone call turns into a chat. Then you "accidentally" run into him at the place you know he goes every week. You start spending some time together, and there's no denying that the spark is still there. Unfortunately, so are all of his bad habits.

Breaking up with a guy is like kicking an addiction— you want to quit because it's toxic, but it's all too easy to fall off the wagon. Here's Lauren's philosophy on setting boundaries and sticking to them.

HOW TO MAKE A CLEAN BREAK LIKE A LAUREN

No breakup is ever easy, but Lauren and Jason's breakup was particularly messy. "In the beginning, we'd have mostly good days, and a bad day every once in a while. But we had so much fun and I loved him so much that the good days were all worth it. Towards the end, it was mostly bad days, and once in a while we'd have a good day."

"In order to be in a good relationship with someone, you have to be okay without that person. I had forgotten what that was like. We were totally codependent. Another person shouldn't complete you, but they should make you feel great about yourself. At that time, neither of us were feeling great about ourselves." Here's a helpful hint: if you're not feeling good about yourself for whatever reason, you're going to have a hard time helping someone else feel good about *himself*.

The peaks and valleys of their relationship began to take their toll on Lauren: "I didn't like the person I had become. I was angry at Jason all the time and it was making me mean and hateful. I knew it wouldn't stop unless I broke up with Jason." Finally, Lauren asked Jason to move out of her apartment and started packing his belongings.

As hard as it was to move Jason out, living without him was just as hard. "At first, I was crying because Jason and I were fighting all the time," Lauren recalls. "Then I was crying because he wasn't there to make me stop." The downside of having intense relationships is that, when they fall apart, they lead to intense breakups. "I couldn't sleep, I couldn't eat. I couldn't do anything. His stuff was still all around, and absolutely everything in my room and around the apartment reminded me of him."

Lauren was faced with the classic problem: she knew she couldn't continue things with Jason romantically, but she didn't know how she could continue without his friendship: "You don't spend every day for a year with a person and then instantly cut them out of your life. I didn't want him to hate me. But after I broke up with him, I thought he was never going to want to talk to me again. I was really scared of losing Jason as a friend."

In the short term, the easiest thing in the world would have been for Lauren to go back to Jason. They had all the same friends and she knew all the places where he hung out, so she could easily have pulled an "intentional run-in" trick. But she knew that nothing long-term would be solved by going back to a relationship that was broken. "He's the person who's comforted you through all your hard times. It makes sense that you'd reach out to him during this hard time, and you forget that he's the one who caused it." A good strategy for moments of weakness: appoint a designated friend to be your watchdog. When you feel yourself slipping, she can remind you that the two of you broke up in the first place for a reason.

"I've learned that nothing good comes from running back to your boyfriend," Lauren says. "There's still too much emotion there, and things get confusing. You get in the cycle of getting back together and back together, but that doesn't do anything to fix the problem. Most of the time, you still end up breaking up for good. All it does is make a bad situation last longer."

"I remembered a saying: 'The one that's worth your tears will never make you cry,'" Lauren recalls.

"Every time I caught myself wanting to see Jason, I just thought of that saying. It reminded me that there was a reason why we had broken up. You don't cry that many tears with the guy you're meant to be with." Lauren resisted the urge and kept her distance from Jason.

Lauren didn't see Jason until several months had passed and the emotion had died down. When they did finally reconnect, they were able to be friends and re-

Heidi's Good Date/Bad Date

Good Date:

"He takes you somewhere meaningful. I wouldn't love Don Antonio's, but I love it because Spencer loves it. It's his place. You get to know a lot about a guy when he brings you somewhere that's special to him."

Bad Date:

"He tries to impress you by taking you someplace fancy and stiff. The place means nothing to him, so he's out of his element. How can you have fun and be yourself when you're out of your element?"

Good Date:

"There's lots of laughter. Laughing is a sign of good conversation, good company, and a good date."

Bad Date:

"Lots of awkward pauses and silences. Making conversation is like pulling teeth."

Good Date:

"He talks about things that you're both interested in. If
a guy wants to find a topic I'm interested in, talking
about me is a good place to start!"

Bad Date:

"He talks about himself. A one-way conversation is
never good. I've been on dates in Hollywood where all
the guy would talk about is his agent, his auditions, and
his career. One guy literally brought his modeling book
to show me pictures of himself!"

● ● ●

member the things that they did love about each other
before they were buried in the complications of a relationship. "I had to make a clean break. I had to give it
some time. It doesn't matter how mature you are, if
you ever want to be friends with your ex, you just can't
do it right away."

When you've been in a relationship for a long time,
it's easiest to make a clean break.

Learning How to Be Single

· ·

One day, you're a part of a couple. You have a ready-made date for dinner, someone to dance with, and when you're feeling depressed, someone to cuddle with on the couch. You have the same friends, the same jokes, and the same iTunes playlist. For the last chapter of your life, you've shared every birthday, every party, and every major life event with him. You're a pair and everyone knows it. Then one day, it's over.

Suddenly, you have to get used to being on your own. Dinner out might require a couple phone calls to friends. A movie date is probably going to be with your roommate. You need to figure out how to be all right by yourself, and not part of a couple, and that includes not staring forlornly at the cute couples you see when you go out. Basically, you need to relearn how to be single.

Of all the challenges you'll be facing on your own, dating is probably the scariest. But with the right attitude, it doesn't have to be a terrifying task or a sad reminder of what went wrong. As our girls discovered, jumping back into dating was not only fun, but gave them a chance to improve upon their past relationships.

HOW TO DUST YOURSELF OFF LIKE A WHITNEY

"There's only one way to get over a bad breakup," Whitney says, "and that's to get back out there."

Whitney remembers her most recent breakup: "When I broke up with my boyfriend of about two years, I had no interest in going out, and I definitely wasn't ready to meet new people. But eventually, I had to quit feeling sorry for myself. I needed to get back out there and I needed my friends to help me do it."

When you've been out of the dating scene for a while, getting back in can be intimidating.

When boyfriends let you down, girl friends pick you up: "Luckily, I have people like Lauren and Audrina in my life, and they knew just what I needed. They insisted on dragging me out. They told me to come over, we all got ready together at their place, and then we all went out. They knew I'd fight them the whole way, but they weren't hearing no."

"I was still pretty shook-up at that point," Whitney remembers, "and I was definitely off my 'Single Whitney' game, so Lauren chose Big Wang's, a laid-back beer-and-chicken-dive bar. She was the first to say, 'We're just bringing you out to look, and nothing more.' Lauren and Audrina understood that I wasn't ready to go out and meet a lot of boys, and no one was asking me to forget about my two-year relationship in one night. They set it up so that I could get out, have a few laughs, shoot some pool, eat some ridiculously caloric fried chicken, and *maybe* talk to a boy."

"As much as I was dreading the thought of being in a crowded bar full of people having a good time while I was still feeling bad about my breakup, a funny thing happened. I started to have fun myself. It was good to be out, and it was great to take my mind off my problems, even if it was only for a few hours. But I realized later that it wasn't the bar, or the boys, or even the chicken wings that cheered me up. What cheered me up was knowing that I had loving friends who wanted to take care of me when I was going through hard times."

It never feels good when a serious relationship comes to an end, but if you're lucky and have good friends, the recovery can be fast. If you're really lucky and have great friends, the recovery can even be fun.

HOW LAUREN GOT BACK IN THE GAME

"For a long time after I broke up with Jason, I couldn't imagine being with another guy," Lauren remembers.

Lauren knew she didn't want to be with Jason, but she wasn't ready to be over him, either. "I didn't want to go out, and I didn't want to meet people. I knew no guy would hold my interest, so I was like 'No more dating! No more boys! No more falling in love!'"

Eventually, Lauren got over Jason, but it was still a long time before she felt comfortable going out as a single girl: "I thought I was just bad at being single.

Even before I started going out with Jason, I hadn't really dated in two years. All of a sudden, I was on my own again with a very rusty set of dating skills."

Happily, Lauren made a full recovery, but it took a lot of work. "I basically trained myself to be single, and to be good at it. I read a lot of books about dating and relationships. I forced myself to go out, and I made myself have fun. Going out and talking to new boys took a while to get back into. Flirting, on the other hand, came back very naturally!"

Lauren remembers her first few dates as a newly single woman: "It's very odd getting back into dating once you've been with one guy for a while. You have to go on a lot of awkward dates before you're really comfortable again. You find yourself struggling for conversation, and the date feels like work. But once you get the bad dates out of the way, you'll be surprised and find you're enjoying yourself. You'll come home from a date and walk through the front door with a smile. That's when you know you're officially back in the game."

So remember, being good at being single isn't something you forget how to do. You may just need to take a refresher course.

SPECIAL
THANKS TO

Lauren Conrad, Audrina Patridge, Whitney Port, and Heidi Montag. Adam DiVello, Sean Travis, Liz Gateley, Tony DiSanto, Sara Mast, Spike Van Briesen, Sandy Cohen, Sophia Rossi, Joshua Harnden, Ashley Perry, Vanessa Hughes, Mel Marin, Lollion Chong, Jennifer Heddle, Jade Chang, and Seth Jaret.